# How to Fly-Fish

# How to Fly-Fish

*Cliff Hauptman*

STACKPOLE
BOOKS

Published by
STACKPOLE BOOKS
5067 Ritter Road
Mechanicsburg, PA 17055
www.stackpolebooks.com

Printed in the United States

First edition

10  9  8  7  6  5  4  3  2  1

*Cover photograph by Fred Bobson*
*Cover design by Wendy Reynolds*

**Library of Congress Cataloging-in-Publication Data**
Hauptman, Cliff.
  How to fly-fish / Cliff Hauptman.— 1st ed.
     p. cm.
  Includes index.
  ISBN 0-8117-3137-5 (alk. paper)
  1. Fly fishing. I. Title.
SH456H352 2004
799.12'4—dc22

                                                                    2004003564

*To the memory of my best fishing partner,*
*HWH*

# Contents

# Introduction

A lot of would-be fly fishers are intimidated by the sport. They encounter someone fly fishing on a stream, survey the load of arcane gadgetry adorning his fishing vest, observe the unfathomable pains he takes adjusting his leader and selecting his flies, and conclude that all the rigmarole is just too mysterious, exhaustive, and intricate for them to ever fathom. Yet, they continue to feel an undeniable attraction to the whole thing—the standing in the water and having such an intimate connection with nature; the graceful curve of the cast line; the meditative, yogalike calm of the exercise. I have lost count of the numbers of men and women who have said to me, "I've always wanted to take up fly fishing, but it seems so complicated. I don't think I'd ever get it."

Paradoxically, they are both right and wrong, and that is what this book is about. You do not have to "get it" in order to have a good time fly fishing, just as you do not have to know a great deal about automotive engineering in order to enjoy driving your car. You do, however, need to know something about a few essentials like steering, braking, and how to turn on the lights and wipers. Fly fishing can be no more complicated. If I tell you exactly what items of equipment you need and what they are for, you can be out fly fishing tomorrow and having more fun than you can imagine.

On the other hand, fly fishing can get as complex and intricate as you want it to. For every aspect of the sport, there are nearly endless layers of intricacy, nuance, and discovery. That is what allows fly fishing to become an intense, lifelong calling, rather than just a pastime.

One of the deterrents for those attracted to fly fishing but intimidated by its seeming difficulty is the way many books approach the subject. They either try to cover all the ground at once, reinforcing the notion that, to learn to fly-fish, you must also learn all the arcane and teeming intricacies that go with it, or they simplify the sport to such an extent that the beginner can appreciate neither the larger picture into which those fundamentals fit, nor the justification for the passion with which fly fishers regard their sport.

What I try to do in this book is to give you both—and a choice. First, I want you to get out there, starting to fly-fish. In order to do that, you need some equipment, and I will tell you exactly what to get. I will also tell you what the equipment is for and why my choices make sense. That is the equivalent of giving you the minimum orientation in how to use your car so you will not kill anybody, including yourself. Chapter 1, then, gives you the list of what you will need.

Subsequent chapters explain each item on the list in a section called "For Starters." There you can learn just enough about what that item does to use it properly on the water right now. If you read only those sections, you will know enough to go out and catch fish on a fly. They may be all you need for quite some time.

Each chapter also contains a section called "Here's Why This Can Get More Complicated." Those sections, when and if you decide to read them, will give you some insight to the ways in which each item can be modified or replaced to address situations and solve problems for which the prescribed item is inadequate. In other words, I will show you how fly fishing can become the endlessly fascinating and complex sport you always thought it was, but not until you want it to be. It is possible to enjoy years of fly fishing without ever altering a single item on the original list or delving more deeply into the sport. It is *very* possible to do so for a few weeks.

So, read chapter 1 and the "For Starters" section of the other chapters, and start fly fishing right away. If you want to learn more and get a sense of the wondrous scope of the pursuit, keep reading the "Here's Why This Can Get More Complicated" sections, or come back to them.

Most of all, have fun, and do not worry about whether you are doing things right. Remember that the way you tell a beginning fly fisher from an experienced one is that when the beginner snags his backcast in a tree, he looks around self-consciously to see if anyone saw him. When the experienced angler does it, he just ties on a new fly. It is not the fly in the tree that brands one as a beginner, it is the lack of knowing that calamity and mishap are normal companions to fly fishing, no matter what one's level of expertise.

# Chapter 1

# What You Need to Get Started

If you have been thinking about getting started in fly fishing and wish someone would just tell you what equipment to get instead of giving you choices you are not yet sufficiently informed to make, you have picked up the right book. The items listed in this chapter are all you need in order to fly-fish for trout. Once you read the "For Starters" section of each chapter in this book, you can take what you learned and the items suggested, put them all together, and, adding only the experience you get by fishing, go out and fly-fish for trout with enough knowledge and equipment to have years of fun.

"But I don't want to fly-fish for trout," you say. "I want to fly-fish for tarpon." Good grief, you are arguing with me already. No matter what type of fish you are eager to pursue, I am recommending that you start with trout on a small stream. I explain my reasons in chapter 8, and all the prescribed equipment is based on that recommendation.

Here are the things you will need:
- a 9-foot, 5-weight graphite rod—the best you can afford (chapter 2);
- a single-action fly reel made for 5-weight line—you can be more economical here (chapter 3);
- a 5-weight, weight-forward, floating line with 75 yards of braided backing—most quality brands are similar (chapter 4);
- a 9-foot, knotless, tapered leader with 4X tippet—get a spare (chapter 5);
- ten assorted flies (a size 8 Bead Head Woolly Bugger streamer, size 8 Muddler Minnow, size 10 Hornberg, size 14 Royal Wulff dry fly, size 14 Adams, size 14 Elk Wing Caddis, size 12 Hare's Ear Nymph, size 14 Pheasant Tail Nymph, size 10 Dave's Hopper, and size 12 Foam Beetle)—buy a few of each if you can afford it (chapter 6);
- a bathing suit or shorts and a pair of sneakers (chapter 9);
- a small box for carrying your flies (chapter 10);

- some fly floatant (chapter 10); and
- a pair of line clippers (chapter 10).

*A Word about Casting*

I make no attempt in this book to teach you how to cast. I do not believe that any book can do it well. That is not to say that there are not good books about fly casting, but I feel that their real value is appreciated only after you already have a little bit of experience with the activity. Nearly the same is true of videotapes and DVDs.

By far, the best way to learn how to cast with a fly rod is to find someone who knows how to do it well and to have that person spend an hour or two showing you how it is done. The instructor can watch you cast, see where you need improvement, make appropriate adjustments to your technique, and show you a few useful variations. Once you get the feel of it and appreciate what is involved in making an acceptable cast, then you can watch some videos and study some books to refine your skill. Do it the other way around, and you may quickly develop some poor habits that an instructor will have a hard time trying to correct.

Do not, however, let anything delay your getting out on the water and starting to fly-fish. If you are lucky enough to know someone who can show you how to cast, acquire from that person just the most basic ability, for now. If no such person is available, watch a videotape or DVD that teaches basic casting, but just enough to get the general idea. In either case, do not wait until you can lay down a perfect 60-foot cast. As soon as you can place your fly three rod-lengths away, more or less in the vicinity you had hoped, with fair consistency, you are ready to fish. Do the rest of your practicing on the water. The worst that can happen is that you make a lot of bad casts and scare all the fish. At some point, though, you will start making better casts and not scare all the fish. Once that lone, fearless, and brain-damaged fish goes for your fly, your casting will improve much more quickly. It always does.

My point is simply that to begin succumbing to the magic of fly fishing, you do not need to cast extremely well. Eventually, you *will* want to improve your casting because you will find that the ability to make pinpoint casts improves your success in catching rising trout, tailing bonefish, and cruising tarpon; that the capability of laying out a 60- or 70-foot cast increases your likelihood of hooking Atlantic salmon on large rivers, or striped bass and bluefish from shore; and that having a repertoire of different casts helps catch all kinds of fish in difficult situations. But I firmly believe that if, for now, you can just get a fly to land 25 feet in front of you, go fish. The rest will follow.

# Chapter 2

---

# Rods

**FOR STARTERS**
**The 9-foot, 5-weight graphite rod**

A 9-foot, 5-weight graphite rod is a good choice for beginning fly fishers. In order to explain why, though, and what that even means, I will have to back up a little bit and explain a few general concepts about fly fishing. Bear with me; this is the easy part.

Most of the lures used in fly fishing have no noticeable weight. Flies are often made of feathers and hairs tied on to relatively tiny hooks. If you tried to cast a typical fly with common, monofilament fishing line, it would go nowhere. In order to cast a weightless fly, fly tackle employs a line that has enough weight to cast, and the line, in its flight, carries the fly to the target.

Because the fly fisher usually seeks to cast his fly with some degree of accuracy and to some reasonable distance, the fly line must be propelled in a controlled way. One does not simply catapult the fly as though launching Jell-O off a spoon in a food fight. Rather, the fly line performs its fly-delivery function by describing a rolling, parallel-sided, horizontal loop, like an elongated U lying on its side. To obtain the energy to create and move such a loop, which usually contains about 30 feet of fly line, the rod must be properly loaded during the cast. That is, the weight of the line, at the critical point in the casting stroke, must flex the rod to the optimal degree so that the potential energy in the flexed rod will be transferred to the line for maximum casting power. Although this is not something you need to worry about at the moment, it helps to explain what a fly rod does and what 5-weight means.

Every fly rod is designed and built to perform best when casting a line of a specific weight. To keep things orderly, rods are most commonly numbered from 1- to 12-weight, lightest to heaviest, and so are lines. The weight of the line you are using determines the weight of the rod you should use. We will get to lines and what determines which weight you

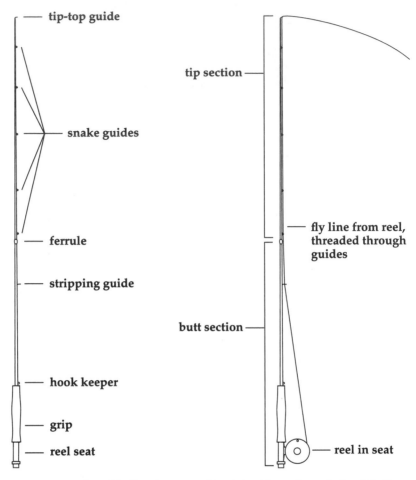

*A typical, two-piece fly rod (left). The same rod (right) with a reel attached and fly line threaded through its guides, ready to use.*

should use in chapter 4. For now, just know that the rod weight should match the line weight.

A *5-weight* rod, then, is one designed to cast a 5-weight line. The recommended *9-foot* length is fairly standard, fly rods most often being offered in lengths of 8½ feet and 9 feet, although longer and shorter lengths are available.

*Graphite*, as opposed to bamboo or fiberglass, is the material of choice. Nowadays, the vast majority of commercially available rods are made of strong, flexible, lightweight graphite. You may, however, be in possession of either a bamboo or fiberglass rod if you have acquired a fly rod through primogeniture, the material depending on how avid an

*During a normal forward cast, the rod is brought forward and stopped, but the line keeps going, unrolling as a continuous loop that ultimately unrolls completely, straightens out, and falls to the water.*

angler the ancestor was. Most ardent enthusiasts owned bamboo; the more casual owned fiberglass. Today, fiberglass fly rods have gone the way of wooden tennis rackets, and bamboo fly rods are expensive and popular with relatively few devotees.

That is all you need to know about rods for the time being. Just be sure the rod is designed for a 5-weight line, is 9 feet long (8½ feet is okay, too), and is made of graphite. All of that information should be printed directly on the shank of the rod, just ahead of the cork grip. This rod will

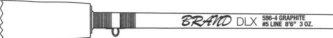

*Notations on a rod's shank often include the name of the manufacturer, the model of the rod, a code number that indicates the rod's specifications (in this case, the 586-4 is a code for 5-weight, 8 foot, 6 inch, 4 piece), the material of which the rod is made, the line-weight rating, length, and the weight of the rod.*

get you started and may last a lifetime as your only fly rod or may quickly become one of many.

### HERE'S WHY THIS CAN GET MORE COMPLICATED

The 9-foot, 5-weight rod prescribed above is all you really have to know for now. With that, you can go out, catch fish, and enjoy yourself immensely for many years without ever concerning yourself with any other complexities regarding fly rods. Eventually, though, if the sport gets a grip on you, you will expand your horizons and, at some point, encounter a fishing situation not particularly suited to that rod. Another way of looking at it is that problems of fishing will arise for which the 5-weight rod is not the right solution, not the right tool. By that time, however, you will have more practical experience and an appreciation of some of the situations for which other rods may be the solution, and you will be glad there are so many subtle variations in available rods from which to choose the precisely right tool.

In addition to line weight and length, fly rods also vary in their action, taper, sensitivity, weight, design, number of sections, and general quality of manufacture. These are all aspects of fly rods that will influence your preference of one rod over another, once you begin to understand why you might want more than one rod. Let's take a look at each factor.

### Line Weight

As explained earlier, fly rods are designed to function best when matched to a specific weight of line. Right away you have a dozen possibilities, from 1-weight to 12-weight, most commonly. The different weights of line are for different fishing situations, species sought, flies used, water conditions, and wind conditions, all of which will be discussed in greater detail in chapter 4. Suffice it to say for now that, in terms of understanding quality fly rods, you should match the rod's line-weight designation to the weight of the line—a 5-weight rod for a 5-weight line, an 8-weight rod for an 8-weight line, and so on.

I specified "quality" rods in the previous sentence because cheaper rods are often less accurately rated. It is not uncommon for an angler using a low-cost rod to find that it performs better when matched to a line one weight heavier than indicated. In such instances, for example, a 6-weight rod may cast noticeably better when loaded with a 7-weight line.

## Length

Independent of a rod's line-weight rating is its length. That is to say that you can find 6-weight rods in lengths of 7, 7 ½, 8, 8½, 9, 9½, and even 10 feet. Some fly rods are as long as 15 feet, others as short as 6. The point is that you have choices, even within line weights.

What dictates your choice of rod length is the fishing situation. First, there is the matter of casting. Small, claustrophobic streams with dense, overhanging foliage demand a short rod of 7 feet or less. You just cannot physically swing a longer rod around in a place like that. On the other hand, on a stream bordered closely *only* by 6-foot alders, a 9-foot rod allows your backcasts to clear the brush. On yet another hand (if you happen to have three), a big western river, a beach, or an open boat allows all the freedom you could ever want for taking advantage of the extra leverage and power of a 9½- or 10-foot rod.

There is also the matter of line handling. As you become more experienced at fly fishing, you will come to realize the need to allow your fly to drift naturally in moving water. In order to rectify a stream's (or the wind's) natural tendency to move your line against your wishes, you will want to be able to flip a drifting belly of line back upstream without causing much commotion down near the fly. That correction is called a mend and is accomplished most easily with a longer rod.

## Action

Rods identical in line weight and length may feel entirely different to cast. That difference, the *je ne sais quoi* that makes you prefer one to the others, is in the rod's action. The subtleties of action preferences are highly subjective. Basically, a rod's action is attributable to where along its length a rod flexes as you cast.

Fast-action rods flex mainly in the tip. At maximum load—that is to say, at the point in the forward or backward cast when the line is exerting its greatest pull on the rod and flexing it to a high degree—most of the bend will be in the endmost one-third to one-half of the rod. By comparison, much of the middle and the entire butt section of the rod will remain fairly straight. Fast-action rods provide power. They cast extremely tight loops that are necessary for long casts. The rod need not move through much of an

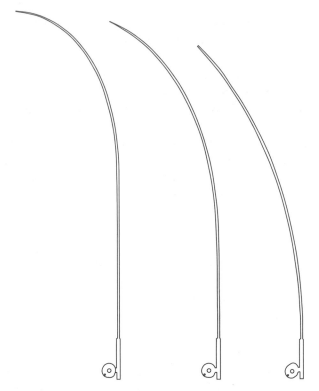

*A fast-action rod* (left) *flexes only towards its tip, while a medium-action rod* (middle) *flexes over more than half its length, and a slow-action rod* (right) *flexes all the way down to its grip.*

arc to provide power to the cast. Accomplished fly casters can take advantage of these traits and be highly accurate as well. Beginners who try to learn to cast using a fast-action rod often end up switching to golf instead. The stiffer butt section of the rod helps fight larger fish.

Medium-action rods show a bend in about two-thirds of their length. Both the tip and midsection flex under load, while the butt remains stiff. This is a kinder, gentler action, to paraphrase a former U.S. president who is also a fly fisher. Because more of the rod flexes during the cast, the casting rhythm is slower, line speed is reduced, and the act of casting is more forgiving of imperfect technique. Medium-action rods perform well over a wide range of fishing circumstances, providing a strong butt for fighting fish while protecting the leader from breaking with its flexible tip. Most fly rods you come across in the sports departments of large, general-merchandise stores are medium-action rods. Beginning and intermediate fly casters do well with medium-action rods.

Slow-action rods flex over most of their length. This action is perfect for small, delicate rods used with very light lines in close-range situations. They also make small fish feel like trophies. Because the entire rod flexes during casting, a slow, gentle casting rhythm is best. Traditional bamboo rods were slow-action, and some anglers who appreciate the advantages of graphite but enjoyed the action of bamboo still prefer slow-action graphite rods.

Naturally, those three actions are not absolute. There are dozens, maybe hundreds, of fly rod manufacturers, and each has its own idea of exactly where fast-action becomes medium-action, and where medium-action becomes slow. In fact, one manufacturer's fast-action rod may seem more of a medium-action when compared to the offerings of a manufacturer that makes really fast rods. Often, manufacturers will print a rod's action on the shank, along with line weight and length. That, however, is usually helpful only in comparison to other rods by the same manufacturer.

Then there is the effect on rod action of the length of line you are trying to cast. Since the line-weight designation of a rod is based on the line-weight designation of the line it is designed to cast, and the line-weight designation of the line itself is determined by the weight (in grains) of the first 30 feet of the working part of that line (again, we will get into this in detail in chapter 4), every rod performs best when you have about 30 feet of line in the air. That is to say that the rod will be performing at its intended action at such times. Coincidentally, much fly fishing takes place at distances of around 30 feet, so everything usually works pretty well.

There are plenty of times, however, when long casts are necessary. You may be confined to the shore of a pond, the bank of a river, or a beach. You may be fishing to particularly spooky fish that will not let you approach any closer than 50 or 60 feet. Or, you simply may be stubbornly unwilling to risk your life by wading into dangerously deep water despite the presence of hungry and eager fish just beyond normal casting range. Situations like those occur more frequently the more you fish. At such times you will find yourself attempting to hold far more than 30 feet of line in the air while you cast, and your rod may suddenly feel unfamiliar, perhaps somewhat limp and "noodley." That is because you have increased the weight of the line by adding to its length. If the rod is normally a medium-action rod tending toward slow, the increased weight of the extra 20 feet of line you are trying to cast will have made the rod flex beyond what you are used to, changing it, effectively, to a slow-action rod. There just may not be enough power in it to cast that much line efficiently.

If you find yourself routinely needing to make casts of longer than 35 feet or so, and your rod feels kind of wimpy when you do, get yourself a faster-action rod or use a line rated at one line-weight lighter than the one you have been using. The problem with this latter solution, however, is that the lighter line will not load the rod properly on shorter casts, and if you find yourself in a situation in which normal-length casts are again preferred, you will feel as though you are fishing with a pool cue.

**Taper**
Although a casual glance at a fly rod reveals merely a long stick that tapers gradually from a thicker base to a thinner tip, the nature of that taper is what influences the action, discussed previously. Even over a given length, say 9 feet, the number of ways a tube of graphite can get from its butt diameter to its tip diameter is quite mind-boggling. Faster-action rods have quicker tapers; slower-action rods taper more gradually. There are progressive tapers, compound tapers, reverse compound tapers, multitapers, and others, all of which are an attempt to shape the rod in such a way that its feel, or action, suits some fly caster, somewhere, fishing under some set of specific conditions.

**Sensitivity**
Your rod's ability to transmit the often subtle sensations of a fish bumping your fly or of your fly bouncing along the bottom or moving through weeds is necessary to your success as an angler. The ways in which materials are combined in manufacture, how they are used in the process, and the actual design of the rod all contribute to a rod's sensitivity or lack thereof. A rod can be so sensitive that you would think it part of your hand, while others cause you to wonder if you are wearing gloves, so little feeling is transmitted to your fingers.

Unfortunately, there is no way to know the sensitivity of a rod until you fish with it. Generally speaking, though, as with most products, well-known rod makers make rods with dependable sensitivity; others are a crapshoot.

**Weight**
This refers to the actual weight of the rod itself, as opposed to its line weight. Although rods designed to cast heavier lines do also tend to be heavier themselves, variations in rod design and materials produce differences in the weights of similarly rated rods. This is true not only among manufacturers, but within lines of a single manufacturer. Just among the various models of 9-foot 6-weights offered by one company, the weights of the rods range through 3.25, 3.5, 3.75, 4, and 4.5 ounces. Go ahead and pooh-pooh the apparently trifling differences, but then come back after

spending eight hours of steady casting and tell me whether you didn't wish at some point that your rod weren't just a hair lighter.

A rod's weight is a function of its design and the materials used in its manufacture. There are numerous ways to manufacture graphite and to employ it in the creation of a fly rod. The materials used to make the reel seat, the way the ferrules are created, the number and composition of the guides all influence the weight of a rod. Always, in the designs of the highest-quality rods, is the attempt to find the ideal balance of power, performance, and weight. Anyone can build a strong rod by bulking up on materials, but its weight will wear out the caster in no time. The art of

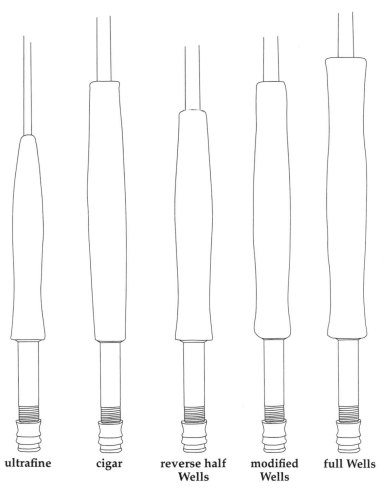

| ultrafine | cigar | reverse half Wells | modified Wells | full Wells |

*A few common designs for cork grips.*

rod building reaches its apex in the strong and durable, yet delicate and lightweight, precision wands available today. That is, at least, until a newer and yet more perfect material is developed. The weight of a rod is often printed on its shank along with the other pertinent data.

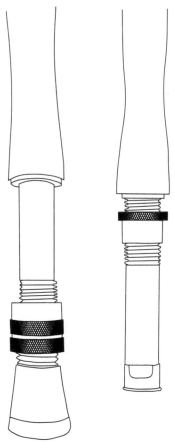

*The rod on the left employs an up-locking reel seat; the foot of the reel fits into a slot below the grip, and the knurled lock is screwed up to hold the reel in place. The rod on the right has a down-locking seat; the reel's foot sits in the pocket on the butt cap, and the lock is screwed downward to hold the reel in. Note the knoblike fighting butt on the rod on the left.*

## Design

Besides the characteristics that influence the way a rod performs are those that affect the way it looks. There are, for example, variations in the design of the cork grip, which most popularly comes in a full Wells or reversed half Wells configuration. The way the reel is held securely to the reel seat, too, may be up-locking or down-locking, depending on whether you seat the foot of the reel in the grip and screw the locks up to it or you seat the reel foot in the butt and screw the locks down to it. Some rods have a bulbous fighting butt that you can hold against your belly as you fight a heavy fish. Some rods have snake guides and some have ring guides. Some rods have a glossy finish; others have a matte finish.

Eventually, if you become a habitual fly fisher, you will meet fellow enthusiasts who actually hold strong preferences for one or another of these features and will gladly expound on the relative merits of their choices. Most fly fishers, however, concentrate on the more important aspects of rod choice and do not sweat such details. In other words, they find a rod whose casting characteristics suit them, and they live with whatever other fine points of design come with it.

## Number of Sections

Most fly rods come in two sections of equal length for ease of transport and storage. The sections fasten together by means of a ferrule, which allows one section to be inserted into the other for a couple of inches, forming a tight and secure connection.

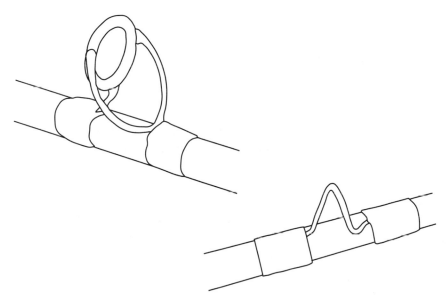

*A ring guide* (left) *is typically used for the first (stripping guide) and last (tip-top) guides on a fly rod. Snake guides* (right) *are usually used in between.*

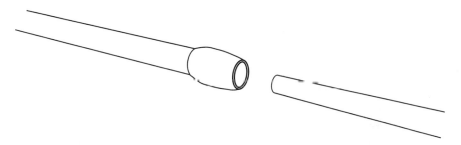

*Ferrules (pronounced "ferals") allow sections of rod to be joined together.*

A few decades ago, pack rods became popular, allowing a hiking fly fisher to carry a tube of only about 24 inches in length, secured to his pack, and containing a full-length fly rod broken down into four sections. This modification was performed simply by cutting a normal rod into short sections and adding ferrules. The result was a rod that no real fly fisher would ever want to use. The problem was that if the original rod, before modification, was a 5-weight, the new travel rod, now stiffened by three additional ferrules, required at least an 8-weight line to put any kind of bend in it. Despite that, it was still regarded by its manufacturer as a 5-weight and labeled as such.

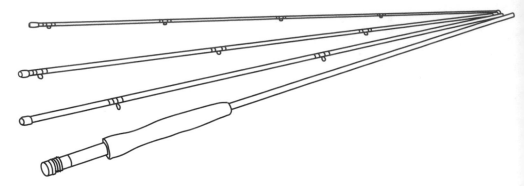

*A 4-piece travel rod.*

Happily, rod manufacturers have gotten a lot smarter and now realize that multisection rods, now called either travel rods or 4-pieces (there are even 5-piece rods, but 4-pieces are more common), must be designed that way from the start, so that they retain the casting characteristics they are intended to have. Fly rod manufacturers have become so good at multi-piece rod construction, in fact, that I and many other fly fishers buy only multipiece models. Since there is practically no difference, nowadays, between the performance of a quality rod maker's 4-piece version and its 2-piece version of the same model rod, the convenience of traveling with and storing the 4-piece model surpasses its slight additional weight.

### General Quality
This is the overall merit of the materials used in the rod's manufacture, the care taken in its assembly, and the general sense of craftsmanship, even among mass-produced rods, that tell you whether you have a product of value. Some points to check follow.

### *The Grip*
Fly rod grips are most commonly made of cork. They are assembled by stacking a number of cork donuts around the graphite shank, gluing them together, and then shaping the resulting mass into a comfortable grip. The grip should appear seamless and flawless. There should be no pits in the cork, no soft spots, no oozing glue residue, no gaps. The grip should appear as a single, uniform entity with a velvety, firm feel.

### *The Reel Seat*
This is where the reel fastens to the rod. It may be made of wood or aluminum. If wood, the seat should be perfectly finished and without chips,

dings, nicks, or—heaven forbid—cracks. It should be made of a durable hardwood, often maple, sometimes an exotic. If made of aluminum, the seat should be anodized and its finish should be uniform and unscratched. There should be no dents or crimps. The tightening clamps, whether friction rings (only on the lightest-weight rods) or threaded, should be perfectly round and should tighten smoothly. The butt cap should be tight and show no signs of loosening.

### Rod Wraps

The guides along the length of a rod are secured by wraps of thread, then covered and sealed with lacquer. There are also usually wraps around the ferrules. The wraps should be completely covered by the lacquer so that a glassy, smooth seal is created; no threads should be exposed. There should also be no cracks in the lacquer, although stress marks may appear after you use the rod for a while.

### Guides

Guides may be either ring-shaped or somewhat S-shaped. The latter are called snake guides. The design of guides used is not an indication of quality; certain manufacturers simply prefer one over the other, although even when snake guides are used, the first guide, called the stripping guide, as well as the tip-top guide are always ring guides. The *number* of guides, however, may be of importance. A quality, 9-foot fly rod should have eleven or twelve guides. Cheap rods skimp on the number of guides, leaving overly long distances where the line may sag and impair efficient casting. Quality guides are made of exceptionally hard metal, like titanium, to withstand the wear of line constantly moving through them. Softer metals will eventually groove and create excess friction that will affect casting distance.

Such are some of the aspects of fly rods that cause the avid enthusiast to never own enough of them. As you can sense by the number of possible combinations of variables, here opens a nearly limitless horizon for obsession.

# Chapter 3

---

# Reels

**The 5-weight, single-action reel**

Most of the time, the function of a fly reel is simply to store fly line, but on those happy occasions when there is a particularly strong fish on the line, the reel suddenly becomes a key element in playing and retrieving the fish.

Single-action fly reels are really very simple devices, the fact that they can be manufactured with great skill, to high degrees of perfection, and at great expense notwithstanding, for they can also be manufactured inexpensively to a level of quality and craftsmanship that is good enough for most anglers.

The single-action reel has a horizontal foot by which it is fastened to the butt of a fly rod, just behind the grip, and thus hangs suspended beneath the rod. From the foot extends a disc that forms one side of the reel, and from the center of the disc a short axle extends. On that axle turns the reel's removable spool, much like a spool of thread with very broad ends, almost exactly as broad, in fact, as the disc attached to the foot. A knob for winding the spool extends out of one side. Because the knob is attached directly to the spool, so that one revolution of the knob causes one revolution of the spool with no gears to multiply the effect of turning the knob, the reel is called *single-action*.

On the opposite side of the reel from the knob—on the disc attached to the foot—there is another knob, smaller than the crank knob, that can only be twisted. That is the knob that sets the drag, the amount of resistance applied to the *backward* turning of the spool. Thus, when a strong fish is on your line, you can adjust the drag to keep the line from breaking by allowing controlled slippage but still create enough resistance to tire the fish.

The broad ends of fly reel spools are usually perforated with small, round holes, not only to provide air circulation around the stored, wet line, but also to reduce the weight of the reel.

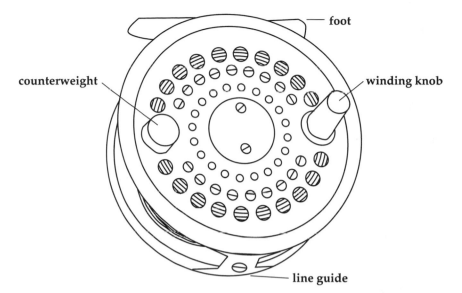

foot

counterweight

winding knob

line guide

*A typical single-action fly reel seen from the removable spool side.*

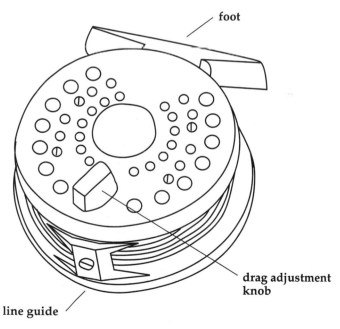

foot

drag adjustment knob

line guide

*The same single-action reel seen from the permanent housing side.*

Reels come in different sizes to accommodate the size of line used. In the prescribed outfit, you will be using a 5-weight line and, therefore, a 5-weight rod (see chapter 2). You should also use a reel made for 5-weight line. Often, depending on the manufacturer, a reel may be described as a 4/5. That means that a reel has a large enough capacity to hold the standard 30 yards of either 4-weight or 5-weight fly line, 75 to 100 yards of backing (see chapter 4), and a few more yards of leader (see chapter 5). A slightly larger capacity reel would be a 5/6, which can handle that same arrangement, but with either 5-weight or 6-weight lines. As with rods, reels are commonly made in sizes to accommodate lines from 2-weight to 12-weight and then some. Ideally, you should use the smallest reel that can accommodate your line, leader, and backing without their bulging over and jamming in the frame; your rod will balance better in your hand, and you will not be waving around any unnecessary weight.

I mentioned that fly reels are mainly used to store line. That is because the reel plays virtually no role in fishing, only in catching. To give yourself enough line for casting, you simply pull line off the reel with the hand not holding the rod, often letting the line just fall onto the water. When you cast, that line goes out the tip of the rod. Upon retrieving your fly, you strip the line back in with that same hand, again letting the loops of retrieved line fall to the surface of the water. Even when you hook a fish, you are likely to have no trouble leading it to your net or hand by holding your rod high to allow the flexing rod to protect your leader, and simply stripping in the line with your free hand while snubbing the line against the grip with the forefinger of your rod hand. The reel comes into play only when a powerful fish threatens to break your leader, and you must relieve the pressure by letting the fish take up the slack line off the water as it runs. Then, using the drag, you play the fish off the reel, bringing him in by cranking line onto the reel and letting him take line back out against the resistance of the drag when the pressure becomes too great.

**HERE'S WHY THIS CAN GET MORE COMPLICATED**
Although when you first begin fly-fishing for small trout and panfish the reel will be among the least important pieces of your gear, once you begin to get into larger, stronger fish and your understanding of the subtleties of the sport becomes more refined, you may find that the prescribed reel no longer meets your needs. As simple as they are, reels comprise a number of aspects that hold infinite possibilities for complication. There are types other than the single-action, a number of different ways to design a drag system, and even a fundamental difference in the style of the hub, or arbor.

**Reel Types**

There are three basic types of fly reels: single-action, multiplier, and automatic.

The *single-action*, described above, is the most popular, especially for catching trout, panfish, bass, and the like. The retrieval crank is attached directly to the side of the spool, and one turn of the crank results in a single revolution of the spool. As simple as it is, many veteran fly fishers never use any other type of reel throughout their entire lives. Many fish do not require retrieval by the reel at all; you simply haul them in by pulling on the line with your free hand, dropping the retrieved line on the water while snubbing the live line against the rod grip with the forefinger of your rod hand. You will be surprised how large a fish you can safely retrieve this way. When the fish is large and a hard fighter, however, you will feel its ability to break your leader if you do not relieve the pressure by letting line slip through your free hand and allowing the fish to run. In that case, it may be best to let the fish take out all the slack line until you can play it off the reel, cranking line onto the reel to retrieve, and letting line slip back out with the reel's drag system. It is also possible to palm the reel to control the fish's run. You do that by applying careful resistance to the spinning of the reel (when the fish runs and takes out line, the reel spool spins backwards) by varying the pressure with which you press the palm of your free hand against the rim of the spinning spool.

The *multiplier* reel is similar to the single-action reel, except that there are some gears between the crank knob and the spool, which multiply the cranking ratio. Instead of one revolution of the knob resulting in one revolution of the spool, one revolution of the knob causes the spool to revolve several times, thus retrieving line onto the reel much more quickly than is possible with a single-action reel. This feature is useful when playing very fast, strong fish like bonefish and Atlantic salmon. Such fish can come straight toward you at great speed, throwing enormous amounts of slack in your line. Until you can take up all that slack and get the fish onto the reel, you have no control at all over the fish and are likely to lose it. A multiplier reel speeds your ability to take up the slack and get the fish back under your control. Naturally, a multiplier reel will be more expensive than a single-action reel of similar quality.

Even faster for taking up slack line is the *automatic* reel. This is a spring-loaded reel that works like a window shade or the power-cord mechanism on a canister-style vacuum cleaner. When you pull out the line, it stays out but puts a load on an internal spring. The more line you pull out, the tighter the spring is wound. When you want to take in slack line, you pull a lever, which releases the spring, and the slack line shoots

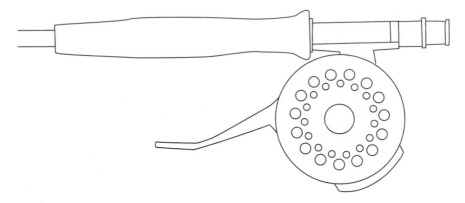

*An automatic reel.*

back onto the reel in a flash. At that point, though, you use the automatic as you would either of the manual reels. Like the multiplier, the automatic increases line pickup so that you have better control of your line when playing a fish. It also increases cost, weight, and the number of things that can go wrong with your reel. But it is mighty handy when you really need it.

**Drag Systems**
Most of the time, you do not need a drag system at all. For normal, small-stream trout and panfish, you will strip the fish in by pulling on the line, and, if the fish fights hard enough, you will let line slip back out through your fingers until you can pull it in again. For larger, stronger quarry, you will play the fish off the reel, and a drag will come in handy.

A reel's drag system controls the amount of resistance applied to the backward turning of the spool, varying the difficulty with which a fish can pull line from the reel and keeping the reel from spinning out of control and spilling line into a tangled heap that will eventually cause you to lose the fish.

Smoothness is the key necessity of an effective drag system: the smoothness with which it overcomes inertia at the start, and the smoothness with which it maintains a constant pressure. When using extremely fine tippets (the monofilament line to which the fly is attached—see chapter 4), sometimes as fine as a hair, a fish's sudden jerk can break the line. The lower the *start-up inertia* of the reel spool, the smoother it will respond to the tug, and the better it will keep the line from breaking. When the drag is set correctly, it, too, must allow the spool to respond smoothly to start up. The drag must also allow the spool to maintain a

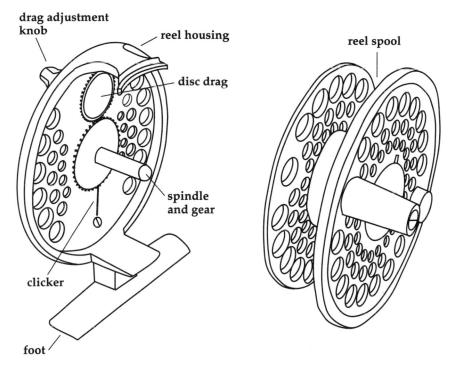

drag adjustment
knob

reel housing

reel spool

disc drag

spindle
and gear

clicker

foot

*A single-action reel with its spool removed, revealing the clicker and disc drag in the housing.*

constant reaction to changes in speed when the fish is pulling line off the reel during long runs. Variations in the resistance of the drag mechanism—especially if it seizes up entirely, as low-quality drags have been known to do—will cause the loss of your fish.

There are three common types of drag systems upon which an infinity of variations are based.

### Ratchet and Pawl

This is the system found in many older and inexpensive reels and is entirely serviceable for most small stream and pond fishing. Similar to holding a stick in the spokes of a wheel, a spring holds a teardrop-shaped pawl against the teeth of a gear, allowing the gear to turn more easily in one direction than the other. Often, the pressure of the pawl against the gear is adjustable, but sometimes it is fixed. Fishing writers often conjure the image of the screaming reel as a hooked lunker rockets away, stripping line from the reel at blinding speed. The scream originally was the sound of the pawl, clicking in the gears at extremely high speed. It is a sound that makes the hairs stand up on the backs of veteran fly fishers' necks, so much so that a clicker mechanism is now actually present in nearly all fly reels, even those using drag systems other than the ratchet and pawl.

### Caliper

This system works like nondisc brakes on a car. A caliper clamps its pads against a surface of the revolving reel, producing drag that slows the outgoing line and tires the fish. It is more finely adjustable than the ratchet and pawl system and adds to the cost of the reel. Many of the better-name manufacturers employ a caliper system in their midprice reels.

### Disc

Most higher price reels have a disc drag. The system is the same as disc brakes on a car: A knob on the reel frame adjusts the amount of pressure a disc-shaped pad exerts on the flat, inner face of the spool. The larger the disc, the smoother and more finely adjustable the pressure. A variety of materials are used for the pad, including felt, cork, and such synthetics as Teflon and Delrin, all of which affect the cost. One common variation of the disc system is the offset disc drag, which introduces a couple of gears between the adjustment knob and the disc.

Regardless of drag system design, most reels offer an exposed rim on the spool so that you can further regulate resistance by adding pressure with the palm of your hand.

### Arbor Size

The arbor is the core or hub of the reel's spool, around which the line is wound. Until relatively recently in the long history of fly fishing, the arbors of reels were all pretty much about the diameter of your thumb. Despite the fact that a number of nuisance shortcomings resulted from that design, it was not until 1986 that anyone tried to do anything about that.

### Traditional Arbors

One problem with a small arbor is that it takes an awful lot of cranking on a single-action reel to take up slack line when there is little left on the reel. Once most of the line is back on the reel, the accumulated line itself has effectively increased the diameter of the spool so that more line is taken up with each turn. But when most of your line is on the water and you must take up slack in a hurry, the small diameter of the traditional arbor affords little help.

Conversely, when a large fish is taking line off the reel against the drag, the spool must turn faster and faster as the diameter of the hub decreases. That is when less aristocratic drag systems become overtaxed and start to bind and apply jerky, uneven pressure, usually resulting in lost fish.

Another minor but irritating product of traditional reels with small arbors is that the end of the fly line closest to the arbor is wound around a narrow hub. Thus, when you strip line off the reel to cast, it can often look as though you have dropped the spiral coils of a Slinky on the water. Line memory causes the coiling to be quite persistent, interfering with casting and line handling.

### Large Arbors
By significantly increasing the arbor size of a reel's spool—that is to say, by increasing the size of the hub around which the line is wound—all of the shortcomings of the traditional arbors are corrected: More line is retrieved faster; spool speed is reduced and rendered more constant as line is taken out by a running fish; and coiling of the line is reduced.

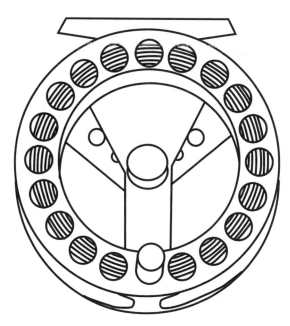

*A large-arbor reel.*

Naturally, though, large-arbor reels are not a panacea because they introduce a few shortcomings of their own.

By increasing the size of the arbor, you naturally leave very little line capacity, unless you make allowances somewhere else. So, you must either increase the overall diameter of the entire reel or increase its width, thus giving back horizontally what you confiscated vertically. Bulk, therefore, is increased either way. Additionally, the wider spools introduce the new retrieval problem of line building up in one spot until it jams against the reel housing. Initially, too, large-arbor reels were more expensive than traditional reels of equal quality. However, that is becoming less and less the case.

Most experienced fly fishers nowadays, unless they are inveterate traditionalists, find that the strengths afforded by large-arbor reels more than offset their weaknesses.

When they were first introduced, large-arbor reels were mainly of interest to big-game saltwater fly fishers. Now, though, large-arbor models are being offered by nearly every reel manufacturer at every price level. Still, however, if you buy gear as an outfit—the rod, reel, and line as a complete, preset package, rather than buying each component separately—the reel is much more likely to be made with the traditional arbor.

### Righty or Lefty?
Most reels are made so that a couple of minor alterations, which can easily be performed by the user, will allow you to change the orientation of the reel so that you can crank with either your left or right hand, depending on which you prefer. Some right-handed anglers like to make their right hand the active one, passing the rod to their left hand after casting with their right, so that the right hand can strip in line or reel if a fish takes the fly. Other righties, like myself, prefer to keep the rod in their stronger right hand all the time, not only for casting, but for playing the fish as well, stripping or reeling with the left. The same applies to lefties. Experience will determine your preference. Try both.

### Color
Fly reels can be made in any color you can think of, although most come in black, silver, or gold. Those who prefer black do so not because it goes with anything, but because they feel it to be less visible and, therefore, less alarming to spooky fish. There may be something to that, but even silver reels with a brushed or matte finish give off so little shine that they may actually be less reflective than the glossy surfaces of some black reels.

Gold seems to appear most often on large saltwater reels that are fished from boats where the quarry are not likely to be spooked.

**General Quality**
Even inexpensive reels should have a reasonable level of quality in their construction, features, and workmanship, while top-of-the-line reels exhibit craftsmanship and quality that rival the very finest of the watch-maker's art.

*Materials*
The best reels are machined from solid bars of aircraft-grade aluminum. Less expensive reels are sometimes made of cast aluminum. Some quality reels are made of graphite, which is lighter still. All of these options are acceptable. Avoid reels made of metals other than aluminum, as they will be unnecessarily heavy, which may seem a trifling issue until around the two hundredth cast of the day . . . if you last that long. Also avoid reels made of plastic, as they are not meant to be taken seriously, even by beginners. There are, however, quality reels that use an innovative system of interchangeable plastic cassettes in place of spools, so that an angler can more easily change the type of line he is using (see chapter 4). Those are quite different from entire reels made of plastic.

*Features*
We have already discussed the drag system, which is one of the most important features of a reel when powerful fish are involved. The best quality reels, for the most part, use disc drags of one form or another, and the larger the surface area of the disc, the better the drag. Well-made reels have drags with very low start-up inertia and constant pressure through-out a long run. They also are designed with an exposed spool rim for palming.

Well-made reels have winding cranks that are balanced by a counter-weight directly opposite on the face of the spool. This ensures that the spool will spin smoothly, without wobbling from the crank handle's weight on one edge.

Reels that are to be used in salt water should have an anodized finish to protect them from corrosion.

All spools should have ventilation holes in both sides, and the higher quality reels will often have ventilation holes in the frame plate as well. The holes not only allow the line to dry quickly but reduce overall weight.

As discussed earlier, reels should be easily convertible for right- or left-handed operation, drag pressure should be easily and accurately adjustable, spools should be readily removable but securely held, and an ability to remove or silence the clicker may be desirable.

*Workmanship*

This is one of those qualities that is partly cosmetic and partly functional. Often, the care taken by a manufacturer over the cosmetic aspects of a reel will reflect the true quality of the workmanship, but it can also serve as a diversion. True quality of workmanship is found in the tolerances with which elements fit together, the lack of any play or wiggle between moving parts that will become amplified, in the heat of battle, to vibrations, wobbles, stutters, and, ultimately, failure of the equipment. Quality is also found in the thought behind the design elements employed to protect the drag system and other innards from sand, dirt, and even water, to which the reel is exposed during normal use. In terms of cosmetics, pay attention to the overall look of the finish and the material used for the crank knob. Knobs may be made of synthetics, antler, bone, or exotic woods.

It is unlikely that if you develop a long-term interest in fly fishing, the reel you start out with will be the only one you will ever need. First, all but the most expensive, custom reels eventually wear out or are rendered useless by sand, loss, or baggage handlers. Quite apart from that, however, is the fact that you will more than likely add a new rod to your collection of gear, and that rod will be designed to handle a different weight of line, thus requiring a different reel to maintain a balanced outfit. So, eventually, you will be making choices based on all the variables discussed above. Like everything else in fly fishing, the sheer tonnage of choices can be either daunting or comforting. Once you gain experience fly fishing, you will begin to understand the limitations of your 5-weight reel and delight in the cornucopia of options before you.

# Chapter 4

# Lines

**FOR STARTERS**
**The 5-weight, weight-forward,**
**floating line with 75 yards of braided backing**

As you have seen in the two previous chapters, it is the choice of line that determines the choices of rod and reel. I prescribed a 5-weight rod, matched with a 5-weight-capacity reel, because you are going to be using a *5-weight line*. But what determines the choice of line in the first place?

I have recommended a small trout stream as your introductory water. Such places hold relatively small fish that will eat relatively small flies. Wind is not much of an issue on small streams. Delicacy of fly presentation is usually a worthwhile goal, but extreme delicacy, especially on a stream that holds stocked trout, is usually not necessary. All of these characteristics are equally true of small ponds you may want to fish. There, bluegills, sunfish, and other small panfish are the warm-water equivalent of small trout.

Given those conditions, the 5-weight line is a good choice because it falls just about halfway along the scale of possible fly line weights from 1-weight to 12-weight. And the types of fishing conditions prescribed here fall just about halfway along the various scales of fishing conditions that we use for deciding the most sensible line weights to use: size and strength of intended quarry; wind conditions; sizes of flies to be used; depth of water; anticipated casting distances necessary; and things like that. A 5-weight outfit—line, rod, and reel—is a good, versatile size for a wide range of fishing. Some feel that a 6-weight is even more versatile. Maybe so, but I tend to prefer going a bit lighter for the beginner; that way, if he decides fly fishing is not his kettle of fish, at least the cause will not be burdensome equipment.

*Weight forward* refers to the line's taper. Most fly lines are about 90 feet in length and change diameter in various ways over those 90 feet. A weight-forward line tapers in such a way that much of its total weight is

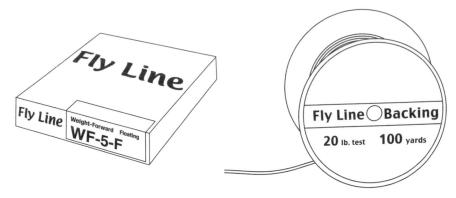

Left: *A box of fly line and its identifying label.* Right: *Most backing comes on a spool like this one.*

concentrated toward the first several feet. That makes a weight-forward line easier to cast.

*Floating* means that it floats, as opposed to sinking well beneath the surface, suspending just below the surface, or having most of the line float while the first few feet sink, which are the cases with other types of line. Floating lines allow you to fish with a fly that also should stay on the surface, and floating lines are much easier to pick up off the water when you want to make a new cast.

The label on the box for this type of line will read "WF-5-F," signifying that it is a weight-forward (WF), 5-weight (5), floating (F) line.

You also need about 75 yards of 20-pound, braided, Dacron polyester *backing*. As mentioned, fly lines are typically 90 to 100 feet long. Most of your casts will be about 30 feet. An expert fly caster fishing for Atlantic salmon or bonefish may routinely make 70-foot casts. Nonetheless, the 90 feet of fly line is not nearly enough when a strong fish you have hooked becomes intent on putting a lot of water between you and it, fast. To avoid running out of line, then, you must attach several yards of thin but strong backing to your reel. Wind that on first, then tie the free end to the tail end of your fly line. On a weight-forward line, the last several feet of the tail end and the first several feet of the head end are very different, although the tips look much the same. The end that you want to attach to the backing usually bears a tag reading, "To reel."

### HERE'S WHY THIS CAN GET MORE COMPLICATED

Think of the line as an important tool with which to solve specific fishing problems: What species am I seeking? How big and strong do those fish get? Are the fish particularly wary? What kind of water do they inhabit? What problems do those waters pose? Weeds? Surf? Fast water? What kind of flies will I be using? Will I be fishing deep or on the surface? Will I have to make particularly long casts? Is casting room restricted? Will there be much wind? Are there extreme temperatures involved? All of those factors affect your choice of line, and that choice, in turn, dictates the rod and reel you should use in order to maintain a balanced outfit.

Fly lines, in order to address the issues raised above, vary in a number of important ways, the most significant being taper, weight, and function, the order of the characteristics by which most lines are identified.

## Taper

The taper of a line describes the way the diameter of the line varies along the entire length of its (usually) 90 feet. The question then arises: why does a fly line have to taper at all? The answer is both simple and complicated.

One end of the fly line attaches to the Dacron backing, a fairly thin, braided line. The other end, as we will see in the next chapter, attaches to a relatively thin leader, usually a tapered length of monofilament. For the fly line to attach to those lines, it, too, must be relatively thin. But in order to cast well, it must also be relatively fat. Clearly, then, in at least two points along its length, the fly line has to taper from thin to fat and back to thin again.

In addition to the practicality of having to attach to other, thinner lines at each end, the fly line also has to perform its casting function to perfection, which means it must deliver a fly to a fish in an accurate yet unstartling manner by transferring energy down the entire length of line so that it straightens out smoothly, flips the fly out ahead of it, and lands properly. That is accomplished by distributing the line's weight differently along its length, depending on what conditions the line has to overcome and how you want it to behave.

One of the important objects of a good cast is that the fly land ahead of the line. That is called turning over the fly. At the end of a cast, while the line is unrolling toward the target, the tip of the line, the leader, and the fly must turn over, all flicking out forward at the last moment so that the fly lands out ahead of all the rest of the leader and line. Otherwise, the line will land on the water before the casting loop has unrolled fully, leaving the fly floating closer to you than some of the line.

The front taper—the taper that changes the line from its skinny tip to its fatter casting weight—has much to do with how the fly turns over. A small, weightless fly with little wind resistance will turn over beautifully

*When a fly turns over properly, it lands ahead of the leader and line (top). When it fails to turn over, you get something like the mess at the bottom, which rarely catches fish.*

when cast by a line with a nice, long, gradual front taper. Without the problems of wind or flies that have poor aerodynamics, you can cast with a graceful, easy stroke, allowing the line to unroll fully and naturally, and the fly will turn over as prettily as you please and land delicately out ahead of the line, causing minimal disturbance. Casting into a stiff breeze or trying to push a big, hairy bass bug or weighted fly through the air requires a bit more power, a more open loop, a less lovely cast, and a line with a faster front taper to make the fly turn over properly.

The physical difference between a fast front taper and a slower one is a matter of just a few feet. Typically, the tip of a fly line—the thin part to which your leader can be attached—is less than a foot long. Over the next 3 to 8 feet, more or less, the line thickens to its widest diameter, a section called the belly, which bears most of the line's weight. If it takes about 8 feet for the line to widen from the tip section to the belly, the front taper is described as slow, the fly will take longer to turn over, and the line will land delicately with the heavier portion farther from the fly. If the line tapers from the tip section to the belly in only about 3 feet, the front taper is described as fast, the fly will turn over quicker and less delicately, and the heavy section is closer to the fly, with the possibility of spooking the fish.

Similarly, fly lines have a rear taper, a gradual narrowing of the line from the belly to a thinner length of line to which the backing can be attached. A longer rear taper allows you to mend line more easily, makes roll casting (a method of casting without a backcast in tight situations) easier, and is more stabilizing for very long casts. As you will soon see,

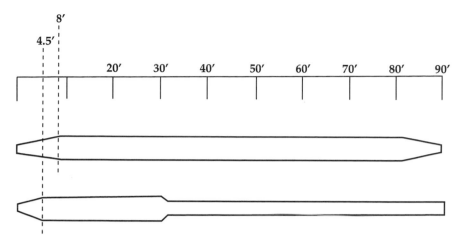

*This schematic representation of a double-taper line* (top) *and a bass taper* (bottom) *shows the relative differences in the lengths of the front tapers and the overall designs of the lines.*

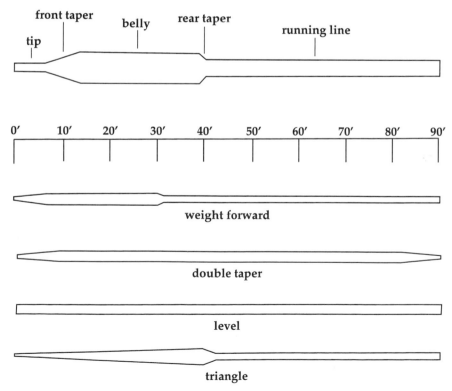

*Schematics of the various fly-line tapers.*

the thinner portion of the line following the rear taper may vary in length quite drastically, depending upon the overall shape of the line as a whole.

To complicate matters, taper has two meanings in describing fly lines. One sense of taper, as you already know, is the thickening of the line at the front taper and the thinning of the line at the rear taper. But a line's taper also suggests its shape, or profile, by describing how and where along the length of the line the belly is distributed. In that sense, there are five basic tapers upon which myriad variations are made: weight forward, double taper, level, shooting taper, and triangle taper.

### Weight Forward

This is the easiest taper for the beginner to cast. Most of the weight of a weight-forward line is concentrated in 20 to 25 feet near the front end. The very tip of the line is thin enough to connect to the leader. Over about 8 to 10 feet, it tapers up (this is the front taper) to a fairly fat line (the belly) that levels out and stays that width for about 20 to 25 feet. Then it once again tapers down over a length of several feet (the rear taper) until it is as thin as it was at the front, holding that width for the remaining 50 or so feet and making it possible to connect it to the backing. This great length of thinner line behind the belly, roughly half the total length of the line, is called the running section of the line. It slips through the rod guides easier than the belly when making long casts and when a big fish is taking out line.

Because most of the weight of a weight-forward line is concentrated toward the tip and, therefore, out beyond the end of the rod during a normal cast, the beginner will more easily experience the loading of the rod during the backcast and will have a better sense of when to begin sending the line forward to perform a well-executed cast. Since successful fly casting is largely a matter of timing, the better you can feel what the line is doing in the air, the sooner and more easily you can develop that sense of timing.

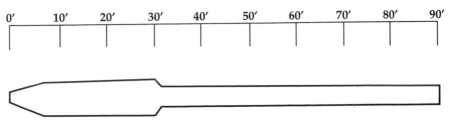

*A schematic of a weight-forward line.*

But there are other advantages to a weight-forward taper that have nothing to do with your level of expertise. Weight-forward designs make casting into the wind easier and they turn over the fly faster, allowing you to cast the big, fluffy, wind-resistant flies that are used for bass, as well as weighted flies.

Because the belly is relatively close to the tip and, therefore, relatively close to the fly, and because weight-forward lines tend to turn the fly over faster, fly presentation with weight-forward lines is usually not as delicate as with the next type of taper.

### Double Taper

A double-taper line has no running section. It tapers up from the tip section to the belly over a few feet, then remains at the belly width for about 75 or 80 feet until it tapers back down over a few feet to the tail section. It is called double taper because it is identical from either end. If the working end of the line gets worn after a time, you can take the entire line off your reel, detach it from the backing, turn it end to end, reattach the worn end to the backing, and have a brand new working end identical in taper to the old one. Not only is this economical, but the double-taper line delivers a more delicate cast than weight-forward line because its taper is long and its belly farther from the fly. It also turns over a fly much more slowly and daintily.

Because of its shape, a double-taper line is somewhat more difficult to cast, mainly because it is harder to feel its effect upon the rod. The beginner may not get a sense of the rod's loading and fail to develop the proper timing. However, it is more easily mended (manipulated upon the surface of the water while it is drifting) and is much easier to roll cast.

Double-taper lines are preferred for streams and ponds where the fish are wary of disturbances, normal-size flies are used, and wind is not much of a factor.

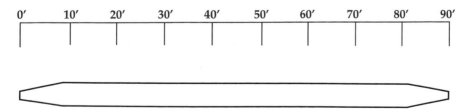

*A schematic of a double-taper line.*

### Level

Very few anglers actually cast with a level line, which has no taper at all; it simply stays the same diameter from tip to tail. Because it lacks a taper, it affords none of the physical attributes that make casting the controlled and predictable accomplishment you hope it to be. Casting with a level line is like throwing a knuckleball. But level lines are comparatively cheap, and the uninformed are often drawn to it as a way of trying out fly fishing with minimal expense. Few, if any, of those unlucky neophytes become attached to the sport.

The most common use of level line is as a running line behind a shooting taper.

### Shooting Taper

A shooting taper is basically the first 30 feet of a weight-forward line that ends in a connecting loop. To that loop is connected as much level running line as you want. What you have, essentially, is a weight-forward line with no rear taper, just a thin running line trailing behind 30 feet of belly.

There is not much subtlety to the cast of a shooting taper, but it goes like a bullet. The head gives it speed and the ability to slice through wind, and the thin running line allows it to shoot through the rod guides with little resistance. Shooting heads are used when the main objective is to cast a great distance.

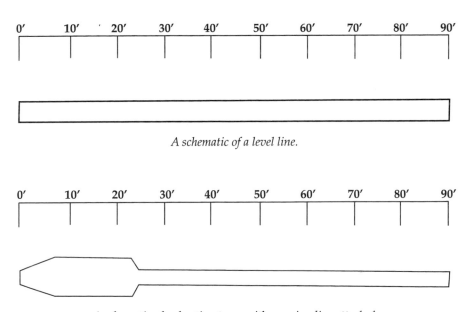

A schematic of a level line.

A schematic of a shooting taper with running line attached.

### Triangle Taper

This is a relatively new taper designed by the late Lee Wulff, one of the icons of fly fishing. The triangle taper starts as a thin tip section, as do most lines, and then continuously tapers to a maximum thickness somewhere between 30 and 80 feet later. Then it quickly tapers down to a tail section to make up the remaining 90 feet. There is no belly; for all practical purposes, the front taper never ends. This unique design is particularly efficient because, at any point along the line, heavier line is always turning over lighter line; there are no level areas. Many anglers prefer this taper for improved line handling and casting, especially roll casting, but it is still not as easy for the beginner to cast as is a weight-forward line.

### Specialty Tapers

Most specialty tapers are subtle modifications to a weight-forward taper. They bear such names as bass bug, pike/muskie, salmon, steelhead, bonefish, tarpon, striper, or big-game tapers, according to the species to which they are meant to be applied, as well as variations of Windtamer, WindMaster, WindCutter, or beginner, novice, startup, LongCast, or distance tapers, according to the purported purpose. Many of these specialty tapers are multipurpose and can easily stand in for each other, as a bass bug taper—an extreme weight-forward taper designed to punch fluffy bass flies through the air—will most certainly be an effective wind-cutting line when used with more aerodynamic flies. Because all these specialty tapers rely on relatively slight differences in the lengths of their front and rear tapers, and their performances in infinitely variable circumstances are mainly subjective, one manufacturer's bass bug line, for example, may be identical to another's tarpon line or another's wind-cutting line or yet another's long-distance line.

Generally speaking, if you have only a double-taper or standard weight-forward line and know you will be needing an additional line for unusually windy conditions or to turn over outsized flies, you will not go

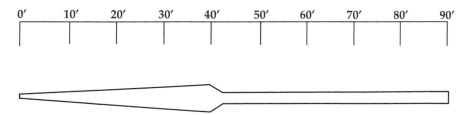

*A schematic of a triangle taper.*

wrong by purchasing the appropriately named specialty taper in the correct line weight for your rod. However, you can undoubtedly use that
same line for other species or applications as well, without an additional
outlay of cash for yet another, nearly identical line with a different name.

### Weight

Line weight was briefly discussed earlier in this chapter, as well as in
chapter 2 on rods. The number, 1 through 12, signifying a fly line's weight
is based on a scale devised by what is now the American Sportfishing
Association (ASA), for the purpose of standardizing line weights so they
can be accurately matched with rods designed to cast them properly. The
first 30 feet of a fly line is weighed, and its weight in grains (within a specific tolerance) is assigned a number. Thus, any fly line whose first 30 feet
weighs between 134 and 146 grains (averaging 140 grains) is a 5-weight
line and may be reliably matched with a 5-weight rod under normal casting conditions. It matters not which manufacturer made the line, what
form its taper takes, or what it is designed to do; if its first 30 feet weighs
140 grains (give or take 6), it is a 5-weight.

The ASA line-weight ratings are as follows:

| Weight | Size (grains) | Tolerance |
| :---: | :---: | :---: |
| 1 | 60 | 54–66 |
| 2 | 80 | 74–86 |
| 3 | 100 | 94–106 |
| 4 | 120 | 114–126 |
| 5 | 140 | 134–146 |
| 6 | 160 | 152–168 |
| 7 | 185 | 177–193 |
| 8 | 210 | 202–218 |
| 9 | 240 | 230–250 |
| 10 | 280 | 270–290 |
| 11 | 330 | 318–342 |
| 12 | 380 | 368–392 |

The weight of line you use is determined mainly by the species for
which you will be fishing, altered perhaps by the size and condition of the
water in which you will be fishing, and fine-tuned by the wind conditions

you will encounter. For bluegills and small trout in a calm pond, for example, a 1-, 2-, or 3-weight line is a good choice. Small trout in a small stream require the same. For trout in a larger stream with faster water and a heavier current, a heavier line, such as a 5- or 6-weight, is needed. You will want to be using a rod with a bit more backbone in order to control fish in such a current, so you must use a heavier line as well. For even larger rivers, whether fishing for trout or smallmouth bass, a 7-weight outfit is appropriate. Largemouth bass, however, tend to want larger, fluffier flies that are harder to cast, and you must often haul these fish out of weed beds. That requires a heavier line still, and an 8-weight is usually the line of choice. Atlantic salmon, steelhead, bluefish, and striped bass, because of their weight and power, require a 9-weight, as do bonefish because of the wind that nearly always hammers the flats where they forage. Permit and tarpon, larger and more powerful still, require a 10-weight, and marlin and other billfish demand the heaviest line available.

So you see that while the choice of line may drive the weights of the rod and reel you will use, there are times when the strength and fighting power of the rod you will need drive the choice of line.

To make matters even more complicated, there are times when you may wish to use a line that is a weight or two heavier or lighter than your rod's rating. When fishing in conditions where extremely short casts are consistently the order of the day, for example, you may benefit by using a fly line rated one or even two weights heavier than the line for which your rod was made. Whenever short casts are the norm, such as when you are fishing a small stream or pond that is only a dozen feet wide, or when trees and brush limit you to 15-foot casts or less, you will not have enough of your fly line out beyond the tip of your rod to load the rod and make accurate casts. Don't forget you will also have at least 7 ½ feet of leader attached to the end of your line, so you will be working with even less line than you think. A heavier fly line will improve the situation. If you have a 5-weight rod, try using a 6-weight line. You may even want to try a 7-weight.

Conversely, there are times when it is beneficial to use a lighter line than is proper for your rod. Although it seems counterintuitive, using a lighter line when fishing in the wind may make casting easier. A lighter line is less wind-resistant and will hold a tighter loop, but you must make up for its lighter weight by using more of it. The trick is to hold in the air, beyond the rod tip, about 10 feet more than the normal 30 feet, thereby having enough weight of line to load the rod properly. This is the sort of strategy that can work quite well, but if it were shown on television, it would bear the subtitle, "This is being done by a professional fly caster.

Do not attempt this at home." In other words, it is not recommended for novice fly casters. You will end up looking as though you fell into a vat of spaghetti.

## Function

You might say that, in dealing with taper and weight, we have been concerned with the horizontal aspects of fly line. A fly line's function puts us in the vertical dimension. How a fly line functions, you see, entails whether it floats or sinks, and if it sinks, how fast, how far, and how much of it. There are four basic categories in this regard: floating line, sinking line, intermediate line, and sink-tip line.

All fly lines are constructed of a core and a coating. The core may be braided nylon or another synthetic or monofilament. The core is a uniform diameter. The material and other characteristics of the core give the fly line its proper degree of stiffness and stretch. The coating is usually some type of flexible PVC plastic with materials embedded in it. Changes in the thickness of the coating provide the line's tapers, while the nature of the embedded materials determines the function of the line. Tiny, air-filled cavities throughout the coatings of some lines cause them to

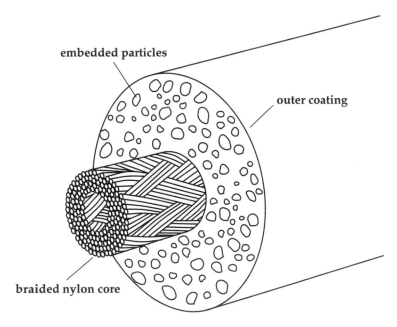

*A cross-section of fly line, showing the braided core and the coating. When the particles embedded in the coating are air balloons, the line floats. When they are tungsten, the line sinks.*

float. The coatings of other lines contain powdered tungsten, which makes them sink. What is interesting and important to remember is that the first 30 feet of a 5-weight floating line and the first 30 feet of a 5-weight sinking line weigh the same.

### Floating Lines

Floating fly lines are available in every weight and taper. They are meant to float high on the water's surface, and some manufacturers add to the coating a hydrophobic chemical that actually repels water, causing the line to touch the surface as little as possible. Floating lines, therefore, are the easiest types to lift from the water when making a cast.

Generally speaking, floating lines are used with floating flies. A floating line, first of all, will not sink and drag the fly down with it. Secondly, when you are casting upstream to feeding trout and your dry fly is drifting back downstream towards you, you do not want your line to be sinking beneath the surface and hanging up on rocks as it moves downstream with the current. Rather, you want it floating on the surface where you can strip it in as it approaches you, high and dry and out of harm's way. Likewise, when fishing for bass in the weeds, you want your line to stay above the snags and tangles.

Floating lines are also used when fishing with sinking flies. Whether on small streams or the shallows of lakes, the $7\frac{1}{2}$-, 9-, or 12-foot leader at the end of your line provides plenty of opportunity for a sinking fly to drift below the surface. Yet, the floating line is easy to lift from the water for casting and, most importantly, can be lifted with minimal disturbance.

Of great importance, too, is the ease with which floating lines can be "mended." This does not mean repaired. To *mend line* means to flip a belly of line back upstream so that it does not drag the fly unnaturally. If

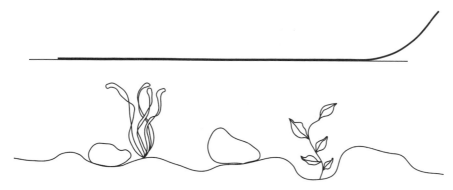

*A floating line sits on the water's surface.*

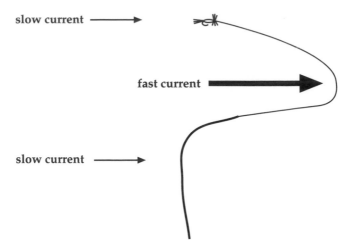

slow current   ⟶

fast current

slow current   ⟶

*Braids of currents in a stream move at different speeds and cause your line to react accordingly.*

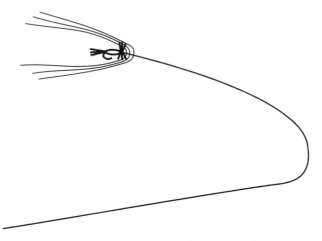

*When a part of your line or leader is drifting at a different speed from your fly, the fly will drag, creating a wake and alerting the fish to its fraudulence.*

you cast across moving water, as in a stream or small river, your line will inevitably span two or more currents moving at different speeds. Your objective, in order to fool a fish into accepting your fly as food, is to have the fly drift as naturally as possible, no faster or slower than the patch of water on which it is riding. Unfortunately, nearly everything in nature is working against that goal, and you will find that some portion of your line is being pulled by a demonic current in such a way that it is headed

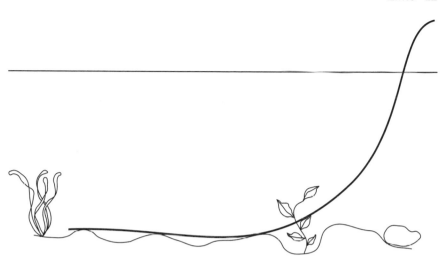

*A sinking line falls to the bottom if currents and obstacles do not prevent it.*

downstream much faster than the rest and is about to drag your fly with it like a water-skier behind a powerboat. Your only hope at such a time is to use your rod to flip the offending belly of line back upstream beyond the fly. Only floating line allows this maneuver.

### Sinking Lines

Although floating lines pretty much just float (if you've seen one, you've seen 'em all), sinking lines can be made to sink at different rates by varying the density of the tungsten powder in the coating. Whether a line sinks at a rate of 4 inches per second (ips) or 6 ips may seem negligible to us, but a fish may not hit a fly falling at the wrong rate. Or, you may be casting from a drifting boat, and if the line does not pull your fly down fast enough, it may not reach the fish's feeding level until you are out of range. The strength and speed of stream currents also affect how deep you can get a fly to sink. Most fly line manufacturers, therefore, offer lines with sink rates that are quite precisely controlled to within less than an inch per second, so that they may have six or seven lines ranging in sink rate from 1 1/4 ips to 8 ips or more. On every box of sinking line, the sink rate is given as a range, such as 2 1/2 to 3 ips. There may also be a descriptive name, like medium fast.

Because sinking lines are nearly always weight-forward, the diameter of the line that is in the water varies significantly from the tip to the belly to the running line. Because the line sinks rather than floats, those variations cause sections of the line to sink at different rates, resulting in a wide bow that

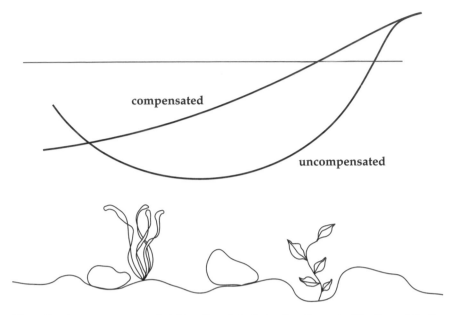

compensated

uncompensated

*The belly of an uncompensated sinking line sinks faster than the rest of the line, while the entire length of a compensated sinking line falls at the same rate.*

jeopardizes the positive, straight-line connection between you and the fly. To remedy this problem, manufacturers may precisely modify the density of the fly line's coating so that the entire line sinks at a uniform rate. Sinking lines given that kind of density compensation will say so on the box.

Sinking lines are useful in a variety of situations. Bass in lakes will often seek deep cover on especially bright days. A fast-sinking line is the only way to consistently present a fly on or near the bottom, which may be 15 feet or deeper. Similarly, when trout are feeding near the bottom in deep, fast streams and rivers, the only way to get a fly down to them is with sinking line, the speed of the current and depth of the water dictating the sink rate you will need to use.

Normally, sinking lines are used with sinking flies, but an effective way to fish for bass that are suspended above the bottom is to use a buoyant fly with a sinking line. The line lies on the bottom while the fly, tethered to the line by a few feet of leader, attempts to rise to the surface. Each time you strip in some line, the fly is yanked to the bottom momentarily and then rises enticingly to the limit of the leader.

Sinking lines are essential tools for the well-equipped angler, but they are hard to lift from the water when casting, more unwieldy to cast than floating lines, and impossible to mend.

*An intermediate line sinks so slowly that it practically suspends just below the surface.*

### Intermediate Lines

These lines, as the name implies, are somewhere between floating and sinking lines. They fall below the surface of the water and sink so slowly (about 1 ips) that, in effect, they suspend. Intermediate lines come in all weights. They are most useful in either salt water or large lakes where wave or wind action will jostle a line floating on the surface. Such jostling quickly throws a slew of slack S curves into the line, and when a fish strikes, there is no longer a taut, straight connection between you and the fish. Hook setting is impaired, too much time is lost in taking up slack, line control is nonexistent, and the fish is gone. By suspending just below the surface, an intermediate line is unaffected by wind and surface chop.

### Sink-Tip Lines

This is the marriage of a weight-forward floating line and a sinking line, where the belly, running line, and both front and rear tapers float and as much as 20 feet of level line ahead of the front taper sinks. Since sink-tip lines, like all fly lines, must conform to the rating system that determines their line weight—the first 30 feet of a 5-weight, sink-tip fly line still has to weigh 140 grains, give or take 6—sink-tip lines tend to have a very peculiar profile. The belly portion of the line is greatly shortened, as is the front taper, and there is a much longer amount of level line ahead of the front taper. Because of the short belly, abbreviated front taper, and (weighted!) long level section, to say that castability is not the number-one priority of sink-tip lines is a hilarious understatement. Rather, the purpose of these lines is to allow you to get a fly as far down as is

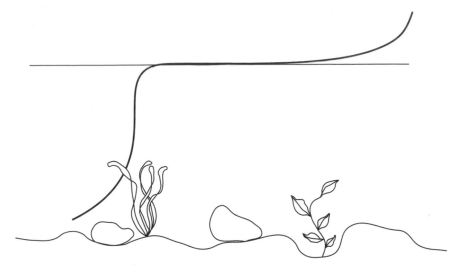

*Most of a sink-tip line floats, while its first few feet sink.*

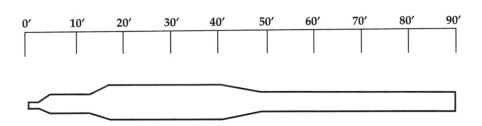

*A schematic of a sink-tip line.*

practical while still retaining a measure of line control—the floating portion can be mended—and ease of lifting the line from the water for the next cast. Sink-tip lines are especially useful on fast streams and rivers where the fly must be delivered near the bottom, but line control at the surface is still essential.

The sinking portion of sink-tip lines shares sink-rate designations with full sinking lines, and sink-tip lines are offered in the same variety of sink rates. The lengths of the sinking portion of sink-tip lines also vary and are available from about 6 to 20 feet in length.

That more or less covers the basics of fly lines. With fly fishing, as with any other pastime in which money is to be made, established manufacturers in the field, as well as upstart, entrepreneurial enthusiasts, continue to offer variations on the mousetrap, replete with claims of vast improvement. Every so often, the claims are true, and the new twist really does make a difference. More often than not, however, their success relies on the proverbial "sucker born every minute."

Now we move on to another piece of line with an importance disproportionate to its length. Take me to your leader.

# Chapter 5

# Leaders

**FOR STARTERS**
**The 9-foot, knotless, tapered leader with 4X tippet**

You cannot tie a fly directly to your fly line. First, the eye of the hook upon which the fly is tied will undoubtedly be too small for the fly line to fit through. Second, the relatively fat fly line, landing right next to the fly, would scare any fish half to death. Third, if you actually managed to stuff the fly line through the eye of the hook and tied the proper knot in it, you would end up with a lump the size of the fly. Fourth, the fly would drift as unnaturally as an anchor.

A leader intervenes between the fly line and the fly. Most commonly, such a leader is a single strand of tapering, clear monofilament. At its thickest end, the end you attach to the fly line, it may be somewhere between .018 and .027 inch—about the thickness of a new penny and just a bit thinner than the tip of the fly line itself. At its thinnest end, the end you attach to the fly and which is known as the *tippet*, the leader may be as thin as .004 inch—about the thickness of a fine human hair.

Commonly, leaders come in lengths of 7½, 9, 12, and 15 feet. Particularly wary fish require the use of longer leaders so that the fly lands gently and as far as possible from the heavier, more alarming fly line. Longer leaders, however, require more casting skill to make the fly turn over properly. Shorter leaders are best for casting in strong winds, for casting especially large or bulky flies, or for casting in tight areas where you must make short casts and need to maximize the length of fly line in use in order to load the rod.

Like fly lines, leaders are tapered in order to smoothly and efficiently transfer the energy of the cast along the unrolling length of line and leader and, ultimately, turn the fly over so that it lands gently ahead of the line. A leader has three sections: the butt section, the taper, and the tippet. The butt section is the thick end, which may make up as much as half the total length of the leader. A long butt section makes a leader easier to cast.

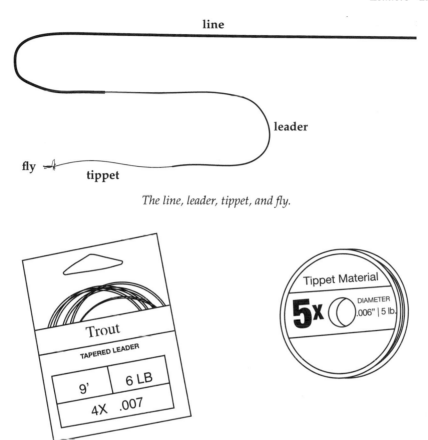

*The line, leader, tippet, and fly.*

*Leaders typically come in clear plastic packets, and tippet material comes on small spools.*

The taper is the section that reduces the diameter of the leader from the butt section to the tippet. The taper may be as short as a quarter of the leader's total length—about 2½ feet in your 9-foot leader. The tippet is the thinnest part of the leader and is typically about another quarter of the total length. You tie your fly to the tippet. The longer and finer your tippet, the more fish you will catch. But long and fine tippets are also harder to cast properly so that the fly turns over and lands naturally.

Leaders are labeled by length and tippet size. Your 9-foot leader is 9 feet long. The 4X tippet is .007 inch in diameter. I have prescribed a 9-foot length because it is a good all-around length to use, especially for one who is not yet a skilled caster. Its 9 feet keeps your fly a good distance from your heavier, more alarming fly line, yet the length is not as difficult to cast as a 12- or 15-foot leader, which is a better choice for wary fish.

Most of the flies you will be using at first will not require the use of a shorter, 7 ½-foot leader.

The 4X tippet is also a good match for the size of flies you will be using. For the most part, you want to use the finest tippet you can get away with because the longer and finer the tippet, the less you will scare the fish and the more naturally the fly will appear. "Get away with" means that you can cast well enough to make the fly turn over properly with that size tippet under the existing conditions. If you cannot, the fly will not act naturally, and your efforts at finesse will be wasted. Then you should use a heavier tippet. Is there any way to make an educated guess about the tippet size you should use once you start straying from my prescription? Yes.

Tippets are rated by an X system, which runs from as heavy as 0X to as fine as 8X. By using the rule of 11, you can figure out the tippet diameter. Subtract the X number from 11, and you have the tippet diameter in thousandths of an inch. Your 4X tippet, for example, is .007 inch in diameter because 11 minus 4 is 7. A 2X tippet is a heavier .009 inch (11 minus 2), while a 6X tippet is a finer .005 inch (11 minus 6). You will note that as the X number increases, the diameter decreases.

Although there are plenty of exceptions, a general rule of thumb in choosing the right tippet size for the dry fly you are using is to divide the size of the fly by 3 (fly sizes and types are explained in the next chapter). A size 12 or 14 dry fly will turn over just fine under most conditions when tied to a 4X tippet. Wet flies of the same size can be used with tippets one size finer (5X).

When you buy a leader, you are buying a single, tapered monofilament line with a butt, taper, and tippet built in. Eventually, however, as you lose flies in trees, weeds, stumps, and, if you are lucky, fish, and as you change flies, the tippet section of your leader will get shorter. Before long, in fact, it will become too short, and your fly will begin to land indelicately and act unnaturally in the water. The solution, if you have money to burn, is to buy a whole new leader. Otherwise, you can buy a spool of tippet material, which is monofilament line of a uniform diameter, rated in the same X system as the leaders. When the tippet section of your 9-foot, 4X leader gets too short, simply tie on a couple of feet of line from a spool of 4X tippet material, and you are back in business. Chapter 7 will show you an easy and reliable way to do that.

### A Note on Connecting a Leader to a Fly Line
There are a number of good ways to attach a leader to a fly line. Most are too difficult for the beginner. If you buy your line in a fly-fishing specialty shop, someone in the shop may make the connection for you. If not, there is an easy and satisfactory way to do it yourself.

*The braided loop is worked over the tip of your fly line like a sock, and then held in place with a plastic sleeve and superglue.*

Buy a package of **braided loops** in the appropriate size for your 5-weight line. These are long, thin socks made of braided nylon. On one end is a loop, on the other, an opening. You work the braided sock over the tip of your fly line and superglue it on. Now you have a permanent loop on the end of your fly line. See chapter 7 for instructions on how to make a loop in the end of your leader and join the two loops.

For now, that is all you need to know about leaders and tippets.

## HERE'S WHY THIS CAN GET MORE COMPLICATED

The proper characteristics of the right leader for any given occasion may well be the most highly debated topic in fly fishing. How long overall; how heavy a butt section; how fine a tippet; the proper proportions of the butt, taper, and tippet sections to each other and the whole; the leader material; the tippet material; and the methods of joining the leader to the line and the tippet to the leader are all variables that can affect the way your fly casts, lands, and acts on or under the water, ultimately determining whether fish will strike it.

Much of the time, it is easy to tell if your leader is not performing properly. If your fly slaps down on the water like the tip of a bullwhip, if it lands amid a tangle of tippet like a meatball on a pile of spaghetti, or if it begins to drag unnaturally the moment it lands, you need to adjust your leader in some way. At other times, leader problems are not so obvious. When fishing with subsurface flies like streamers or wet flies, a too-heavy or too-short tippet may be preventing your fly from attaining the proper depth or achieving a natural action. In any case, a sustained inability to get strikes from interested fish may well be an indication that your leader is in need of modification. The intricacies of leader expertise can fill a book of their own, but I offer the following orientation as a peek into the abyss.

### Knotless Leaders

The leaders I have described so far are single strands of extruded, tapered monofilament. Typically they are sold in packages of one to three leaders per package, and they are labeled to indicate their length, tippet diameter, breaking strength, color, and the type of fish or water for which they are designed.

The most common lengths are 7½, 9, 12, and 15 feet. The longest lengths are necessary on clear, slow waters in which stealth and delicacy are of the utmost importance. Shorter lengths—7½ and even 6 feet—are most often used in wind, rough waters, and when casting heavy or wind-resistant flies.

Tippet diameters are given in X numbers, typically from 0X, which is the thickest, to 7X (rarely 8X), which is the thinnest. Trout leaders in the 7½ - and 9-foot length nearly always come in the full range of tippet diameters. The longer leaders—12, 15, and 18 footers—usually are available only in the finer tippet sizes from 4X to 7X, since their purpose is finesse. Very short leaders, necessary for turning over large or bushy flies, usually come with only heavier tippets, from 0X to 4X. Some specialty leaders, such as those for bass, salmon, and saltwater species, are labeled by breaking strength rather than X number.

The breaking strength of a leader is expressed in pounds. It signifies the amount of pressure the leader can stand, when wet, before it breaks. Although tippet X numbers have a direct relationship to breaking strength, the relationship is not universally reliable, for while a 4X tippet of the Nifty Leader Company's Trout-o Nylon Leader is sure to have a higher breaking strength than its 5X Trout-o Nylon Leader, it may not necessarily be stronger than its 5X Trout-o Super Strong Leader or the 5X Trout/Panfish Leader made by the Whoopee Leader Company.

As a general rule of thumb, however, consider the relationship of X number to breaking strength in the neighborhood of the following:

| X number | Breaking strength (in pounds) |
| --- | --- |
| 0 | 12 |
| 1 | 10 |
| 2 | 8 |
| 3 | 7 |
| 4 | 5 |
| 5 | 4 |
| 6 | 3 |
| 7 | 2 |

As I mentioned earlier, heavier leaders made for bass, salmon, and saltwater species are usually rated only in breaking strength—10, 20, 30

CLEAR
*Striped Bass*
SALTWATER TAPERED LEADER
8ft          10lb

*Most heavier leaders for large game fish display breaking strength instead of X numbers.*

pounds, etc.—partly because there are no X numbers for the higher breaking strengths.

Leader color, which may be indicated on the package, is most commonly clear, green, or a reddish-brown motor-oil color, all of which are
intended to be as unobtrusive as possible in the water, and all of which
have their proponents. Conversely, there are leaders that come in bright,
fluorescent orange or green for maximum visibility so that you can see
them in low light situations. Just be aware that these different colors exist;
do not inadvertently buy a fluorescent leader when you want to be cryptic.

Labels on leaders also usually bear the name of the type of fish for
which the leader is designed. This makes choosing a leader easier,
because many variables—length, butt diameter, and breaking strength—
appropriate to fishing for a particular species are decided for you. If you
know the species you are after, you only have to consider the choices
available for that species. Bass leaders, for example, usually do not come
longer than 8 feet; tarpon and billfish leaders are, on average, even
shorter. Leaders for toothy fish, such as bluefish, barracuda, pike, and
muskies, may come with heavy mono or wire tippets. Leaders designed
for specific species may also have specific taper characteristics that help
turn over the types of flies typically used for that species.

## Knotted Leaders

Unlike the single, continuous, tapering strand of the knotless leader, knotted leaders are made up of several level pieces of monofilament knotted together. Each successive piece is a smaller diameter than the one before it, thus forming a leader that tapers from its butt section to its tippet. The casting characteristics of a knotted leader can be easily changed by increasing or decreasing the length of any section of a particular diameter. Knotted leaders can be bought ready-made, labeled with the same information as knotless leaders. Most users of knotted leaders, however, build their own.

Since every different fly pattern, weather condition, and casting idiosyncrasy can alter the way your fly turns over and lands on the water, a leader tailored to the immediate situation can be very helpful, especially when you are casting to extremely wary fish. Many anglers, therefore, build their own leaders according to specific formulae for particular flies and conditions. One typical formula for building your 9-foot 4X leader might go as follows: start with 36 inches of .021-diameter leader material for the butt section. Knot to that a 16-inch piece of .019 to start the taper, then 12 inches of .017, and 6 inches each of .015, .013, .011 (0X), and .009 (2X). Finish with a 20-inch tippet of .007 (4X).

Some anglers feel that the butt section should be as thin as possible to assure the best possible transfer of energy from the line to the leader. Too thin, however, and the leader-to-line connection forms a hinge instead of a nice gentle curve. You may want to see what happens in the above formula if you start with a butt section of .018 instead of .021 and make it 42 inches long instead of 36. Then follow with a 36-inch length of .017, 24 inches of .015, 18 inches of .013, 12 inches of .011, 6 inches of .009, and a 20-inch tippet of .007.

There are hundreds of formulae, covering leaders for still waters, rough waters, windy conditions, long leaders, short leaders, dry flies, weighted flies, and on and on.

A few basic rules of thumb are these: Start with a butt section and taper down to a tippet; make each successive piece shorter than the

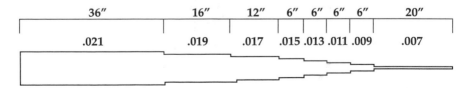

*A schematic representation of the knotted leader formula.*

previous piece, except for the tippet; don't drop down more than two or three thousandths at a time.

**Braided Leaders**

One of the more revolutionary introductions to leader design in the past several years is the braided leader. These are tapered leaders made out of many strands of woven nylon. They come in a variety of lengths and are meant to be used as a permanent butt section. In other words, if you want a 9-foot, 4X leader for your 5-weight line, you buy the appropriate 9-foot braided leader, which is actually about 6 feet of tapered braid with a loop at each end. You make a loop-to-loop connection with the thicker end to your fly line, and you make a loop-to-loop connection of the thinner end to about 3 feet of normal, mono tippet material, bringing the total length to 9 feet. The 6-foot braid remains attached to your line, and you can change tippets—from about 4X to 7X—as needed.

The advantages of braided leaders are that they make it quicker and easier to change tippets over a wide range of sizes, without having to alter the rest of the leader. In addition, they lack memory, so they do not need to be straightened after they have been on the reel for a while. Because they are braided, they have more stretch and are less likely to break when suddenly shocked by a strong fish. Their suppleness also allows them to drift more naturally on the water.

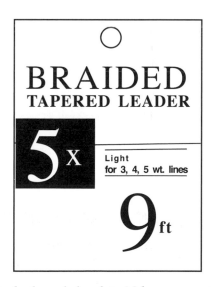

*Braided leaders come in clearly marked packets. Make sure you get the right size for the fly line you are using.*

Disadvantages include their ability to collect water in the interstices of the braid. When you cast over wary fish, the spray from the braid can be a problem. The greatest drawback, however, is especially pertinent to beginners. Beginning casters will often experience what are euphemistically called *wind knots.* These are tight overhand knots that form in your leader during a cast when the top of your casting loop droops over the bottom part. Experienced casters get them, too, every once in a while. When these form in a normal, mono, tapered leader, they can usually be picked out with the point of a hook, leaving only a slight kink at the spot. With braided leaders, however, these knots are almost impossible to pick out without tearing individual strands of the braid, thereby weakening the leader permanently.

## Materials

Complicating the matter of leader preferences among fly fishers is the plethora of leader materials. Not only does the nylon-based monofilament commonly used for leaders come in a variety of colors, all claiming to be the end-all in invisibility, but it comes in a range of stiffness and suppleness that leader aficionados prefer for different sections of their leaders, thus providing infinite subtleties in performance. My going any further into this labyrinth would result in a book that would not only scare you away from fly fishing, but from reading as well.

The one leader and tippet material, besides the standard nylon-based monofilament, that is worth noting, however, is fluorocarbon. This monofilament material is more invisible, abrasion resistant, and stronger than the traditional monos. It is also much more expensive.

For fish with teeth or especially rough mouths—bluefish, tarpon, barracuda, pike, muskies—a short length of wire or *shock tippet* is often added between the tippet and the fly. Shock tippet is usually very heavy monofilament, 12 inches or shorter, that will not be easily cut while the fish is being played.

So far, we have explored a number of elements of fly fishing that matter only to the angler. Now it is time to delve into a subject that actually matters to the fish.

# Chapter 6

# Flies

**FOR STARTERS**
Size 8 Bead Head Woolly Bugger streamer, size 8 Muddler Minnow, size 10 Hornberg, size 14 Royal Wulff dry fly, size 14 Adams, size 14 Elk Wing Caddis, size 12 Hare's Ear Nymph, size 14 Pheasant Tail Nymph, size 10 Dave's Hopper, size 12 Foam Beetle

Flies are nearly weightless lures, usually made from feather, fur, hairs, or synthetic materials tied to a hook. They attempt to imitate things eaten by fish, often with remarkable specificity. They are called flies because they often represent aquatic insects, but they may also emulate small fish, mice, crayfish, worms, ants, and things that do not actually exist but might look like food to a fish.

There are hundreds, perhaps thousands, of fly patterns, with names as inventive as their designs. Some are meant to stay on the surface of the water (dry flies) and others are meant to sink (wet flies, nymphs, streamers). Some patterns are specific to a color, while others have color variations. Most adhere to specific recipes of materials. All come in a range of sizes.

The size by which a fly is designated refers to the size of the hook on which it is tied. The smallest hooks have the highest numbers. In the United States, only even numbers are used. A fly the size of a gnat—as small as this hyphen (-)—would be about a size 28. As the numbers go down, the flies get larger, all the way down to 0 and beyond. The next size larger than 0 is 1/0 (pronounced one-aught), then 2/0, 3/0, and so on, getting larger as they go.

The ten flies I have prescribed are among the most versatile I know. With them, you can catch a wide assortment of fish in fresh water, but mainly trout and panfish. The size 8 Woolly Bugger, however, will most certainly catch good-sized largemouth and smallmouth bass.

The sizes I have prescribed for each pattern are compatible with the fish you will be seeking at first (and maybe forever) and the tippet size you will be using, for the most part. However, this is not an exact science. In keeping with the premise of this book, I have suggested those sizes to make it easy for you to get started, so you can just go out and buy what you need without any confusion or ambiguity. In the case of these flies, though, you can safely go with one size either larger or smaller without any problem. That means that if you go into a store looking for some size 14 Adamses and all they have left are sizes 12 and 16, either will be fine. That goes for all the prescribed flies.

The **Bead Head Woolly Bugger** is a remarkably useful fly. The bead causes it to sink, so it is used as an underwater fly that imitates any number of aquatic creatures—leech, insect nymph, crayfish, minnow, tadpole—depending on how you make it behave. It can be fished in still as well as moving water. In the latter, cast it across and slightly downstream, keeping a tight line as it is swept below you. Then strip it back upstream with short jerks. In still water, cast it out and strip it back, pausing between each strip to allow it to fall on a tight line. Black is an excellent color for Woolly Buggers, but you may want some in brown and olive green as well.

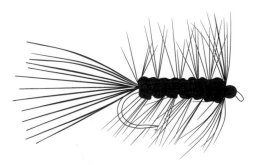

*The Bead Head Woolly Bugger. Its sinuous tail is made from the feathers of the marabou stork.*

*Muddler Minnows* are made partially of deer hair, which, when treated with a fly floatant (see chapter 10), allows this fly to float very nicely and resemble a frog, mouse, or large bug. If untreated, it will eventually sink and imitate an insect nymph or a type of minnow called a sculpin. That makes the Muddler an immensely versatile fly as well. Dry, it can be cast near lily pads and draw strikes from bass. Wet, it makes an excellent trout fly that may be fished much the same way as the Woolly Bugger. Muddlers come in a variety of colors and variations of materials, but you will not go wrong with the standard pattern in a natural tan deer-hair color.

The **Hornberg** is made entirely of feathers and looks like a tiny fish. It swims underwater and is a killer trout fly. Fish it across stream

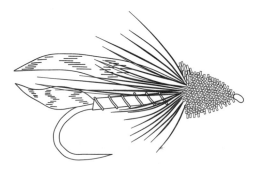

*The Muddler Minnow's tail and wing are made of turkey feather, and its head is clipped deer hair.*

and down like the Woolly Bugger and Muddler, but keep in mind that it is not weighted and does not absorb water, so very fast currents will not allow it to sink much. Use it in gentler currents and still water. Although there are color variations of the Hornberg, stick with the standard natural whitish color for now.

*The Hornberg is made from the flank feathers of a mallard duck.*

The **Royal Wulff** is a dry fly that, when treated with floatant, rides very high on the surface and is very easy to see, even in fast water. It imitates no real insect and is known as a **search pattern**. While many dry flies are intended to replicate specific species, search patterns tend simply to look buggy in a highly nonspecific way. They are useful in locating fish that are not actively feeding on anything specific but are willing to make a pass at a potential meal if one goes by. Royal Wulffs are always the same design and combination of colors. Their white wings make them easy to spot, so the beginner can see when a fish has taken it.

*The Royal Wulff, like most traditional dry flies tied to resemble mayflies, sports a stiff tail, upright wings, and a stiff hackle collar made by winding a rooster feather around the shaft of the hook. The hackle, which radiates like the spokes of a wheel, gives the impression of legs and helps the fly sit on the surface film.*

The **Adams**, on the other hand, resembles any number of aquatic insects, especially several species of mayflies, mosquitoes, and gnats. It is one of the most commonly used dry flies because it can represent so many different insects that trout may be eating at any particular time. They are often hard to see on the water because they are a combination of gray and brown materials. Like the Royal Wulff, the Adams must be treated with floatant in order to keep it on the surface. Both of these dry flies are commonly fished upstream. As they float back towards you, strip in the slack line at the same speed it is moving, so as not to cause any unnatural movement of the fly. When a

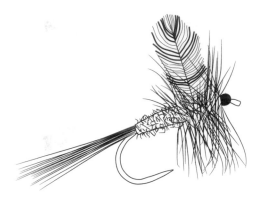

*The Adams, another traditional dry fly, also has upright wings and a dense hackle collar.*

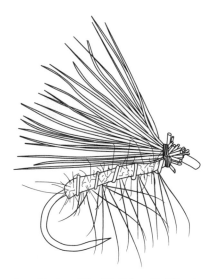

*The splayed hairs of the Elk Wing Caddis give a fluttery appearance.*

fish hits, hold the line and lift the rod. Dry flies may also be fished across stream and even downstream, but you will need to develop excellent line handling skills to avoid drag.

Another extremely useful dry fly is the *Elk Wing Caddis*. As its name implies, its wing is made of elk hair, which helps it to float pretty well for a while without floatant. The Elk Wing Caddis is fished much the same way as the other two dry flies, but because it imitates a caddis, a type of aquatic insect different from those represented by the Wulff and Adams, you may provoke strikes by skittering it across the surface of the water to imitate the behavior of adult caddisflies. Elk Wing Caddises come in a variety of colors, including tan, brown, green, black, and white. Stick with tan or brown for now.

The *Hare's Ear Nymph* and the *Pheasant Tail Nymph* both represent the immature, underwater form of mayflies. They imitate no particular species, but are general, all-purpose nymphs. The Hare's Ear is always tan because it is always made from the fur on a hare's ear. The Pheasant Tail is always dark brown, being made from the brown barbs of a ring-necked pheasant's tail feather. One or the other will almost always be pretty close in appearance to common nymphs in the water you are fishing. Because real nymphs live near the bottom of streams and ponds, the artificials should be allowed to sink as deep as possible. Cast them upstream and across, and let them drift down and sink as they go. Then strip them back upstream in short, quick jerks.

Grasshoppers and ground beetles do not live in the water, but
they live nearby and often fall in.
When they do, fish feast. ***Dave's
Hoppers*** and ***Foam Beetles*** represent such treats. Flies that imitate
nonaquatic insects are known as
terrestrials and, as in this case, are
most often fished on the surface.
Foam Beetles, of which there are
several types, float well because
they are made of foam. Squeeze
them out like a sponge every so
often, and they will float just fine.

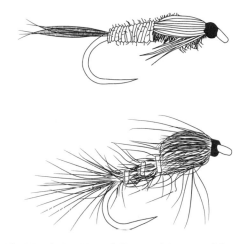

*The Hare's Ear Nymph* (bottom) *is tan and fuzzy,
while the Pheasant Tail Nymph is dark and sleek.
These two flies, in various sizes, imitate the
nymphal stage of a wide variety of mayflies.*

Dave's Hopper is a specific grasshopper pattern, of which there are
several, and has a head made of
deer hair, like the Muddler Minnow. A bit of floatant helps it stay
on the surface. Both of these flies
are excellent panfish lures. Cast
them out on the surface of a pond
and strip them in with little jerky
pops, allowing them to sit still for
several seconds in between tugs.
They can also be fished as dry flies
on streams, where they will be
taken by trout and smallmouth
bass. While Dave's Hopper is
always the same pattern, Foam
Beetles come in many colors. If you
get only one color, get black, but
you might want to pick up some in
green, yellow, or red, too.

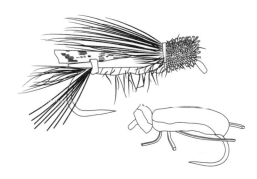

*Dave's Hopper* (top) *and the rubber-legged Foam
Beetle* (bottom) *belong to a group of flies called terrestrials, which imitate insects that do not actually
live in water but often fall into it.*

## HERE'S WHY THIS CAN GET MORE COMPLICATED

You can fly-fish for just about any species of fish you wish to pursue. Different species of fish, however, have different eating habits, live in different environments, and eat different creatures. Even members of the same
species may have different menus in different parts of the country. Yet,
there are artificial flies designed to tempt each of those species in all those

endless variations at any particular moment of their lives. There are flies specifically for trout, imitating every creature in a trout's diet and every stage of those creatures' life cycles. There is a long tradition of tying beautifully ornate flies just for Atlantic salmon. There are flies mainly for bass. There are flies for a wide variety of saltwater fish, from the striped bass, bluefish, bonito, and tuna that patrol the inshore waters of the eastern seaboard, to the tarpon, permit, and bonefish found on tropical flats, to marlin and sailfish in the blue waters of the Gulf Stream. Essential to your understanding of the value and appropriateness of the flies you will need is an appreciation of the differences in how the fish you are after live, what they eat, and how they feed.

Some species of fish are notoriously opportunistic in their eating habits. Bass, for example, typically lurk in dense cover and inhale any hapless creature that will fit in their cavernous maw. Other species, notably trout, tend to be highly selective in their eating habits, keying in on a specific prey to the exclusion of all others during a particular feeding period. These distinctions have evolved as the result of the quite different habitats in which bass and trout live.

In the warm-water lakes favored by largemouth bass, the shallow weed beds teem with an enormous diversity of tasty and nourishing living things. Many of them are in no particular hurry, and there is no current to sweep them away. Bass can be deliberate and eclectic in their feeding habits. Frogs, fish, crayfish, insects of all kinds, snakes, mice, and even birds are on their menu. All they have to do is wait in ambush in the weeds, under a sunken log, or beside a rock.

In the cold-water streams where trout live, a very different dynamic is at work. The water is moving, and individual items of food carried by the current are available to feeding trout for a very short time. Although many of the food items are similar—crayfish, minnows, and aquatic insect larvae—trout and bass live in different worlds. It is the lives of the aquatic insects of trout streams that make the biggest difference, for those are the primary food source of trout, generally speaking. (Many of these insects do appear in lakes and ponds, where they are eaten by bass and other warm-water species, and trout in streams do eat other creatures. But the insect life of streams is so important to the lives of trout that the entire activity of fly fishing grew out of the relationship.)

**Trout Flies**
In particular, three types of aquatic insects—mayflies, caddisflies, and stoneflies—are the players in this pageant. Each of these insects shares a life cycle that comprises a relatively extended nymphal stage that is lived

entirely underwater and a short-lived adult stage that transpires in the air, often on the water's surface. Although all three types of insects appear very different from each other, they do share the honor of being the primary food for trout in the underwater stages, the above-water stages, and the transitional stages in between. To make matters much more complicated, however, there are dozens of different species of each type, all with their own size, coloring, behavior, shape, and schedule of development. And to add further difficulty, when the trout in a particular stretch of stream are feeding on an abundance of a specific stage of a specific insect, it is usually impossible to interest them in anything else.

At such times, trout fishing is at its most challenging, interesting, and exciting, and the angler's skill at matching the hatch comes into play. To understand what that means, you must have some knowledge of the insects, their life cycles, and how artificial flies relate to all of that.

### Mayflies

There are more than 700 species of mayflies in North America. Each begins its life as a nymph, living underwater. Some species cling to rocks, some to weeds, some actively crawl around on the bottom. Some prefer sandy or gravelly habitats, some muddy, and some weedy. Sizes vary from tiny to a couple of inches. Colors include black and nearly every shade of brown, yellow, and green. Some species are solid and some are patterned. Some species spend only a few weeks in the nymphal stage, while others spend years.

At some point in its life cycle, each species of mayfly transforms into an adult within its nymphal skin. This usually occurs at a very specific

*An adult mayfly* (top right) *and a mayfly nymph* (bottom right) *and flies that imitate them.*

time, with thousands of individuals of a given species transforming nearly at once. They then rise to the surface of the water, where they shed the old skin, called the *shuck*, and emerge as winged adults. But they do not fly yet; rather, they float on the surface, their cloudy wings held together pointing skyward over their backs like tiny sailboats, and they drift downstream on the current until their wings dry. Fly fishers refer to this stage as *the hatch*. Soon the mayflies fly to the nearby bushes and await one more change. These *duns*, or subimagoes, will not eat because they have no mouths. They are meant only to mate and die, and that process will take place within the next few hours. They will not live long enough to need a meal.

Although the duns are winged, they are not yet sexually mature adults. While resting in the streamside bushes, they will undergo one final transformation in which they mature sexually. Their subimago skin splits and they now emerge as imagoes, or true adults, called *spinners* by fly fishers. Their form is much the same as when they were duns, but now their wings are crystal clear and the abdominal markings are more intense. Now they are ready to mate, and they rise from the bushes in a swarm over the stream, males and females together. The males mate in the air with the females, who then drop to the surface of the water to deposit their eggs, where they lie spent in the surface film. Fly fishers refer to this stage as the *spinner fall*.

Any particular species of mayfly in a given section of the stream may perform this drama with dependable regularity each day for a week or so. That means that while some individuals are emerging from underwater as duns, others of the same species, who emerged the day before, perhaps, are falling to the surface as spinners. Other species may be hatching at the same time. The air above the stream may contain a blizzard of mayflies, and the water below may be boiling with feeding trout. But those trout are feeding only on a particular species at a particular stage of its cycle. That may be the nymphs, just as they are reaching the surface; the duns, as they float along, waiting for their wings to dry; or the spinners, spent in the surface film. And because a high level of specialization, at any given time, is the most efficient way to take in the most food—if the fish keys in on a specific set of characteristics of a known food during a time of plenty, it does not have to waste time evaluating each item individually—the trout can make the most of the occasion by ignoring everything that fails to match those specific keys. For the fly fisher, this means that you must determine what the fish are eating and use a fly that looks and behaves closely enough to be accepted. Form, color, size, and the way it drifts all come into play.

In order to lend some system of management to the potential chaos of these hatches and spinner falls, specific fly patterns have been established to represent specific species of mayflies, as well as specific stages of those species and, in some cases, even each sex of those species. Over the years, however, fly tiers have come up with new ways to imitate wings, legs, and bodies, so that while these traditional patterns are still popular, variations have also been developed. So even some of the traditional patterns have several variations of style while maintaining the basic characteristics of the original in form and color.

One of the first mayflies to hatch from some eastern streams in the spring is *Epeorus pleuralis*, once known as *Iron fraudator*. The dun stage of this insect is imitated by a dry fly called the Quill Gordon. When a hatch of *E. pleuralis* is taking place and the trout are rising to eat the drifting duns, you must tie on a Quill Gordon of size 12 or 14 if you hope to have any luck at all.

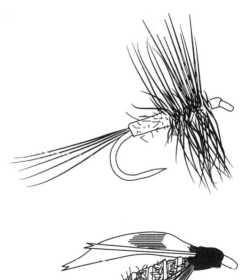

*Ephemerella subvaria* is a mayfly that typically hatches at the same time or just after *E. pleuralis*. A dry fly called the Hendrickson is the traditional imitation of the *E. subvaria* dun female, while the Red Quill imitates the male. Trout can be so selective as to feed only on males or only on females, so it is possible to meet with failure while fishing a Red Quill during an *E. subvaria* hatch if the trout are feeding only on females.

There are hundreds more dry-fly patterns that imitate the dun and spinner forms of mayflies. There are also wet flies, which imitate the underwater stage as the dun breaks out of its shuck on its way to the surface. Traditional patterns for wet flies resemble the dry flies that imitate the same species, but their wings are down over their backs and they are tied on hooks made of heavier wire and materials that allow them to sink.

*The American March Brown dry fly (top) imitates the mayfly* Stenonema vicarium *as a dun. The March Brown wet fly (bottom) imitates the same insect during the brief stage when it has just emerged from its nymphal shuck and is making its way underwater to the surface of the stream.*

Often, they bear the same name as their dry counterparts but with Wet appended. The fly that imitates the emerging female *E. subvaria*, then, is called the Hendrickson Wet.

Nymphs of various designs obviously are meant to imitate the nymphal stage of mayflies, among other aquatic insects, which we will get to. Occasionally an artificial nymph will have a name that indicates the species it represents. You may, for instance, come across a nymph actually called a Hendrickson Nymph. More commonly, though, artificial nymphs are given names that describe the materials from which they are tied. You are already familiar with the Hare's Ear Nymph and the Pheasant Tail Nymph. A nymph's name will also indicate whether additional weight has been added to it, so it will sink faster and deeper. There are also, for example, Bead Head Hare's Ear Nymphs on which you will see a metal bead at the head, and Weighted Hare's Ear Nymphs that have lead wire wrapped around the hook under the body material.

Not all mayfly patterns imitate an actual species of mayfly, however. The Royal Wulff, with which you are familiar, is tied as a mayfly pattern—erect wings and a stiff tail and hackle collar—but it has no natural counterpart. Such flies, usually high-floating, brightly colored, and highly visible, are called *attractor flies* or *search patterns*, for they are used when there is no actual hatch taking place, but when trout will likely eat something that gives the impression of a mayfly, should one happen to drift overhead. Other attractor flies based on mayfly patterns include the Humpy, Irresistible, and Renegade.

### Caddisflies

Adult caddisflies are mothlike aquatic insects that, like mayflies, spend most of their lives underwater in an immature stage, transforming into winged adults that mate and lay eggs. There are more than 1,200 species in North America.

The caddisfly larvae resemble thin versions of the grubs you may find in your lawn. Most, however, are rarely seen naked, as most species build portable cases for protection. Some species make their cases of sand and gravel, some use tiny twigs, and others use other forms of vegetation. Some species spin silken nets between underwater stones to catch bits of food that are drifting in the current. At some point in their development, the larvae pupate for a short time within a sealed cocoon and then emerge as winged adults that swim to the surface, run a short distance upon the surface film, and then take to the air. As with mayflies, these hatches occur as a widespread event in portions of streams and provide a significant feeding opportunity for trout. Mating may or may not occur in a

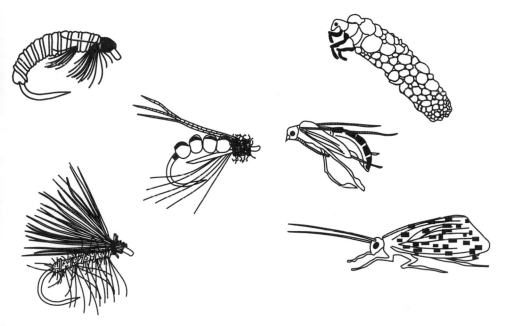

*A caddis larva in its case* (top right), *an emerging caddis pupa* (middle right), *and an adult caddis* (bottom right) *with corresponding imitations.*

swarm, depending on the species, but the females of most species return to the water's surface to lay their eggs.

Adult caddisflies hold their wings tentlike over their backs when at rest. Artificial flies that imitate caddisfly adults, therefore, have wings that lie down over their backs. Most imitations do not have names that correspond to actual species, but are named for their inventor, the materials of which they are made, or their color. The Elk Wing Caddis, with which you are familiar, is so named because its wing is made of elk hairs, giving it flotation and a fluttering look, even when it is sitting still. Unless otherwise indicated, the Elk Wing Caddis usually refers to the tan, natural-colored version. There are also Brown Elk Wing, Black Elk Wing, Green Elk Wing, Yellow Elk Wing, and White Elk Wing Caddis, because this all-purpose caddis can be used to match many different species that are those colors. Thus, you can use an Elk Wing Caddis to match the hatches of many caddisfly species, as long as you have the right color and size. Other popular adult caddisfly patterns are the Henryville Special, Goddard Caddis, and Caddis Humpy. As with the mayfly patterns, there are attractor patterns for caddisflies, such as the Royal Trude and Stimulator, both of which tend to be more colorful than any natural caddisfly.

There are many generalized patterns for immature forms of the caddis-fly, as well, but fly fishers have found that trout will feed selectively on a variety of intermediate stages and anomalous conditions of caddisflies. There are flies that imitate the different types of cases, with the larva's head and legs poking out one end; larvae that have lost their case; larvae ready to pupate; adults emerging from their cocoon with the shuck still attached; adults with malformed wings; adults at rest; and adults with their wings fluttering. And all those come in a variety of sizes and colors to match whichever species of caddisfly the trout are eating at any given time.

### Stoneflies

The third major group of aquatic insects important to fly fishers is the stoneflies. The adults are elongated and narrow and fold their wings one atop the other, flat along their backs. They look somewhat like cock-roaches, to which they are related. They range in size from about a $1/4$ inch to over 2 inches. Their nymphs superficially resemble those of mayflies, but possess small wing pads and lack the feathery gills mayfly nymphs usually exhibit along their abdomen.

Here again the nymphs spend all their time underwater and provide an important food source for trout. Unlike mayflies and caddiflies, how-ever, stonefly hatches are not significant trout-feeding events, for the nymphs usually climb out of the water, up plant stems or rocks, before transforming into adults. Thus, the winged adults do not gather on the water's surface, as do mayflies and caddisflies.

That is not to say that there are no flies imitating stonefly adults. Female stoneflies return to the water to lay their eggs, and when they do

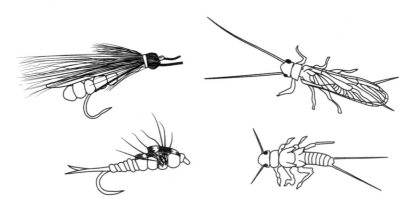

*An adult stonefly* (top tight) *and a stonefly nymph* (bottom right) *with their imitations.*

so in great numbers, fly fishing with dry flies that imitate stonefly adults can be excellent.

Stonefly dry flies and nymphs are usually given names that indicate their designer or their materials, but nearly always include the word *stone*. Many of the nymph imitations look much like the imitations of mayfly nymphs, but some are among the most realistic patterns, looking remarkably like a real insect. Although not specifically designed to do so, the Woolly Bugger, in an appropriate size, makes an excellent stonefly nymph imitation.

Because several species of stoneflies emerge all year, even in the dead of winter, stonefly imitations, both nymphs and dries, make good early-season flies.

### Other Aquatic Insects

Although usually not as important to fly fishing for trout as mayflies, caddisflies, and stoneflies, artificial flies that imitate other aquatic insects abound, as they should, for trout eat nearly all of them at one time or another. Mosquitoes; various water beetles, like backswimmers and water boatmen; water striders; midges; dobsonflies, whose larvae are hellgrammites; dragonflies; and damselflies all spend one or more stages of their

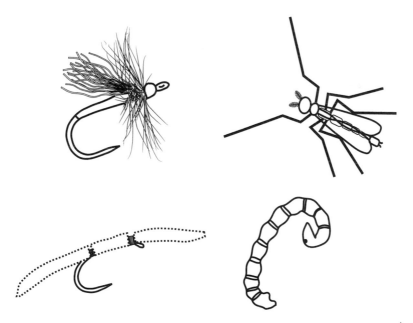

*An adult midge* (top right) *and a midge larva* (bottom right) *and the flies that imitate them.*

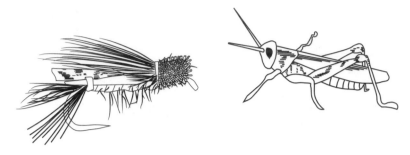

*A grasshopper* (right) *and its imitation.*

lives in water, and the aquatic stages of various species of each of those creatures are imitated by artificial flies. Midges, in particular, can be significant players in a trout's diet, for although they are tiny, they can occur in enormous numbers. Midge nymphs, which look like tiny worms and live underwater, are popular subsurface flies, and imitations of the adults are fished as dry flies. In both cases, the largest midges are usually a size 18, and they get smaller from there, commonly as tiny as size 26. There are also species of tiny crustaceans, called scud, that are an important trout food and common fly pattern.

### Terrestrial Insects

You already know that some fly patterns, like Dave's Hopper and the Foam Beetle, imitate insects that do not actually have any aquatic stages but whose normal activities often cause them to fall into ponds and streams. Besides numerous grasshopper and beetle patterns, there are many popular cricket and ant patterns that are fished as dry flies. During periods when there are no particular hatches occurring, trout will become opportunistic and snap up hapless terrestrials.

### Minnows, Leeches, and Crayfish

Flies that imitate fish are known as **streamers**. Trout eat small fish as a regular and significant part of their diet. The Muddler and Hornberg flies are classified as streamers. So is the Woolly Bugger, even though it is not supposed to imitate a fish, necessarily. Clearly, though, it can resemble some sinuous swimming creature, such as a leech, and although it can also be used as a nymph imitation, as I mentioned earlier, its slender shape, method of use, and the way it is tied place it among the streamers in most fly lists.

Flies that imitate crayfish are also effective in trout streams in which those crustaceans occur. These, too, are usually listed with the streamers.

*A black-nose dace* (left) *and the streamer of the same name.*

Typically, to better imitate the naturals, crayfish flies are weighted and are meant to be fished on the bottom.

Streamers, with very few exceptions (I explained earlier that Muddlers can be treated to float), are fished as wet flies, below the surface. They are most often cast across stream and down, allowed to swing in the current until they are directly below you, and then stripped in with quick, short jerks. Trout will most often hit on the swing or as the streamer is being stripped in.

Some of the most popular, traditional streamers are the Mickey Finn, which is yellow and red and used as a search pattern; the Black-Nose Dace, which does actually imitate a common minnow; the Gray Ghost, which imitates a smelt; and the Black Ghost, which imitates a general-purpose minnow.

Many streamers are made from long, narrow feathers tied parallel along the hook to give them a fishy shape. When streamers are made from the long hairs of a deer's tail, they are called *bucktails*.

Those are the most important types of flies for trout fishing. Many flies used for trout are effective for other types of fish as well, notably panfish. Bluegills and other sunfish will readily hit dry flies, foam beetles, nymphs, and very small streamers. Yellow perch will most definitely chase nymphs of all sizes, as well as wet flies and streamers. In ponds and lakes, cast your fly out, let it sink (or sit quietly on the surface if it is a dry fly), and retrieve it with short, slow strips.

**Bass Flies**

Although such flies as Woolly Buggers and Muddlers in larger sizes are very effective for largemouth and smallmouth bass, there is a category of flies made specifically for bass fishing. These are called *bass bugs*. Made

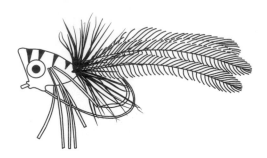

*This floating bass bug is made of balsa wood and feathers and sports rubber legs. Note the strand of heavy monofilament acting as a weed guard.*

of materials that naturally float, such as deer hair, cork, and foam, bass bugs tend to be robust flies that create a bit of a disturbance to attract the attention of a hungry bass. Many have flat faces that pop or gurgle when retrieved. Bass bugs often do resemble bugs, but they just as frequently tend to be froglike or altogether fanciful. Bass are usually not very picky about realism. If a thing seems alive and will fit in its mouth, a hungry bass will usually strike at it.

Because bass bugs are often most effective when cast into holes in lily pad beds, against fallen logs, or alongside stumps, they are often tied with some kind of weed guard to prevent the fly from hooking anything except fish. Weed guards are never 100 percent effective, but bass fishing would be entirely miserable without them.

There are also a number of underwater flies tied specifically for bass. Some of these, like sliders and divers, float at rest but dive when stripped in. Others are meant to sink and stay there. Large streamers of a variety of color combinations are effective on bass. Weighted streamers, like Clouser Minnows and other bucktails, are popular bass flies. Crayfish imitations are especially effective on smallmouth bass. There are even flies that imitate night crawlers.

Bass flies and bass bugs tend to be in the range of about size 4 to as large as 2/0 or 4/0. Most are named to indicate the material of which they are made, the creature they are designed to resemble, or the person who first came up with the design. The Hair Frog and Whitlock's Mouserat are good examples. Some also bear names that describe their action: the Dahlberg Diver, the Hair Popper.

**Saltwater Flies**

Striped bass, bluefish, bonito, and albacore are the fish most sought by inshore anglers on the East Coast. Because all of these species are predatory on small, schooling baitfish, such as sand eels, silversides, mackerel, and menhaden (also called pogies and bunkers), the flies most often used for all four species are much the same. Commonly in sizes 1/0 to 4/0, the Clouser Minnows, Deceivers, Baby Bunkers, Tinker Mackerel, and an assortment of sand eel imitations are the flies of choice. Colors of these flies often match those of the naturals—white below and black or dark green above—and usually contain materials such as Mylar and tinsel that flash like the scales of small fish. At other times, Clousers and Deceivers in bright, attractor colors work best. Most of these flies are designed to swim underwater, sometimes just inches below the surface, but there are floating flies for these species, as well. Skipping Bugs, which are cork- or balsa-bodied flies with tails of feather or bucktail, ride on the surface and pop and skip erratically as they are quickly and jerkily retrieved.

*The Clouser Minnow* (top), *which is weighted, is tied to swim with its hook riding up so it will not snag the bottom. The Deceiver* (bottom) *is made of feathers, bucktail, tinsel, and peacock herl.*

Tarpon, which look like large, stainless steel herring and can attain a weight of 200 pounds, are also popularly caught on flies. Tarpon flies nearly always have "Tarpon Fly" in their names and are used specifically and exclusively for tarpon. They more or less represent needlefish, upon which tarpon feed, and are typically tied in sizes ranging from 1/0 up to 4/0.

Bonefish, silvery fish shaped like the locomotive of a high-speed train, feed in schools on tropical flats. They root small crabs and

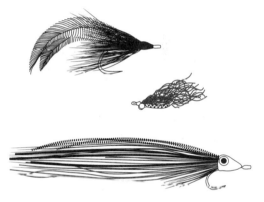

*A tarpon fly* (top), *a Crazy Charley* (middle), *which is one of the more popular bonefish flies, and an 8-inch offshore fly* (bottom) *for marlin and sailfish.*

shrimp out of the marl on the bottom. Most bonefish flies, therefore, imitate small crabs and shrimp and are weighted to sink quickly. They are tied in sizes ranging from about 8 up to 2, with names like Jack's Fighting Crab and Joe's Grass Shrimp. But the best-known bonefish flies are the Crazy Charley and Gotcha, which do not look much like anything.

For offshore species like marlin and sailfish, there are extremely large floating flies, some made of feathers nearly a foot long, with popping, cork heads. These are often fished by dragging a large, feathered teaser behind the boat. The teaser carries no hooks. When a marlin or sailfish comes up to eat it, the teaser is continually pulled from its mouth until the fish is enraged to the point where it will kill just about anything. At that point, the teaser is quickly hauled in, and the fly fisher casts the popper, typically tied on a 6/0 hook, out in its place. This is why 12-weight fly rods are made.

This orientation by no means exhausts the types of flies available for fishing. There are plenty more saltwater species—redfish, sea trout, dolphinfish, barracuda, amberjack, wahoo, shark, roosterfish, pompano, jack, and dozens more—with specialized flies. There are also many more freshwater fish with flies tied just for them—Atlantic salmon, steelhead, carp, grayling, pike, muskellunge, arctic char, and many more. But you now have an understanding of the abundance of flies available for the fish you are most likely to seek, as well as an appreciation for fly fishing's potential as a pursuit without end. What is interesting, though, is that, although unlikely, you could fish quite happily for years to come using only the ten patterns I prescribed at the beginning of this chapter. You could also, as many fly fishers do, get into tying your own flies. And that is a whole other book.

# Chapter 7

# Knots

**FOR STARTERS**
**A few useful knots**

It would be hyperbolic to say that knots are as important to fly fishing as they are to rock climbing, but I will have made my point. The importance of knots to your success in fly fishing is entirely disproportionate to their size, cost, and technical complexity. Yet, there are only four knots that I think you absolutely must learn to tie right away, and one of them is not actually a knot.

**The Reel Knot (for tying your backing to the spool of your reel)**
1. Tie a simple overhand knot in the end of the backing.
2. Pull the knot tight.
3. Loop the line around the spool. Using the end of the line containing the knot, tie another overhand knot around the main part of the line.

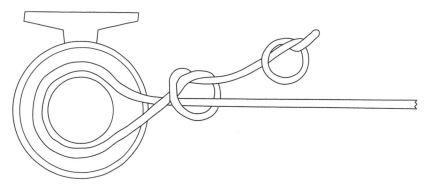

*Reel knot.*

4. Pull the knot tight.
5. Pull steadily on the main line until the knot tightens around the spool. Then keep pulling until the first knot jams up against the second knot. Trim the end.

**The Double Surgeon's Knot (for forming a loop in the ends of your leader and tippet . . . or any line, for that matter)**

1. Double the end of the leader for 2 or 3 inches.
2. Tie a simple overhand knot in the doubled end, but do not tighten it down.
3. Insert the doubled end through the overhand knot.
4. Lick the knot and snug it up slowly and evenly. Trim the end.

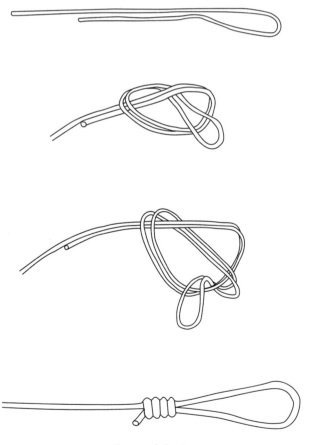

*Surgeon's knot.*

**Joining Two Loops (for connecting your leader to your line and your tippet to your leader)**

1. Insert the braided loop on the end of your fly line entirely through the loop in the fat end of your leader.
2. Insert the thin end of your leader up through the braided loop.
3. Pull the thin end of your leader and your fly line in opposite directions until the loops interlock.
4. To add a tippet section to your leader, make a loop in the thin end of your leader and one in an end of the tippet material, using a double surgeon's knot (above). Insert the loop in the thin end of your leader entirely through the loop in your tippet. Then insert the other end of your tippet up through the loop in the thin end of your leader. Pull the tippet and leader in opposite directions until the loops interlock.

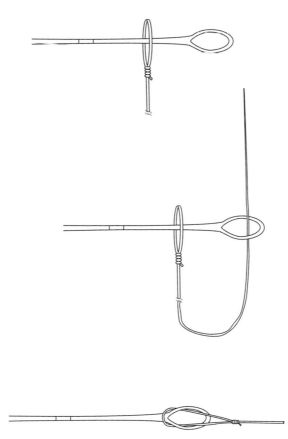

*Making a loop-to-loop connection.*

**The Clinch Knot (for tying your tippet to a fly)**

1. Holding the fly in your left hand, thread about 4 inches of tippet through the eye of the hook. With your left thumb and forefinger, squeeze the fly and line firmly so the line does not slip through the eye.
2. With your right hand, hold the main part of the tippet taut while winding the short end around the main part of the tippet exactly five times with your thumb and forefinger.
3. Poke the end back through the first loop, nearest the eye, and grab it with your left thumb and forefinger while still holding on to the fly.
4. Slowly and steadily pull on the main part of tippet, and draw the knot tight against the eye of the hook. Trim the end with your clipper.

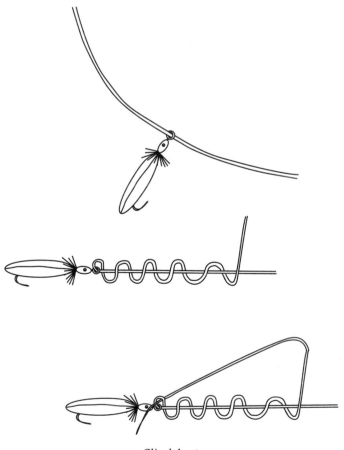

*Clinch knot.*

## HERE'S WHY THIS CAN GET MORE COMPLICATED

For every operation in fly fishing—attaching a fly to your tippet, joining lengths of leader together, attaching a leader to your fly line, attaching your fly line to your backing, and forming a loop in the end of a line—there are at least four or five (sometimes ten) possible good, strong, and reliable knots designed for the purpose. Each has its pros and cons and its zealous advocates among fly fishers. Their main differences tend to be in such characteristics as how easy they are to tie with cold fingers, in poor light, or when dozens of frenzied trout are feeding all around you and may disappear at any moment; how unobtrusively they slip through rod guides when a hooked fish is taking line off your reel at a blazing speed; and how much weeds and pond scum they tend to collect. Many excellent books are dedicated to fishing knots, so I will not go into them in depth here. But you may want to look into some of the following:

For joining sections of leader together, other than by the loop-to-loop method that I have recommended, is the *blood knot*, a popular, attractive, and reliable knot that requires a good bit of digital dexterity. The *Albright knot* is also popular. For attaching a leader to fly line, when not using a braided loop connection, are the *nail knot* and the *needle knot*. For tying a fly to your tippet, popular favorites include the *improved clinch knot*, the *turle knot*, the *Jansik special*, the *Palomar knot*, the *Crawford knot*, the *Duncan loop*, and the *Homer Rhode loop knot*. One of my favorite knots, from an aesthetic point of view, is the *Bimini twist*, which is for putting a large loop in the end of a line. Tying it involves the use of your leg.

# Chapter 8

# Waters

**FOR STARTERS**
**A small, local trout stream**

Just about every state in the United States has either stocked trout streams or streams in which native trout still thrive. These vary from shallow rivers running through open meadows and pastures to woodland brooks enclosed by overhanging trees. It does not much matter what kind of trout stream you choose, as long as it holds trout and the water is flowing.

Although you may want to put in some time on a pond or even a lawn until you can lay out a reasonable cast—a cast in which your line and leader straighten instead of landing in a pile, and your fly lands with at least a modicum of delicacy, close to where you intended it to go—a small trout stream is a good place to make your fly-fishing debut.

The combination of trout and moving water is the key. They force you to cast accurately, handle your line competently, and learn to achieve a drag-free float. Once you learn these fundamentals on a trout stream, you will have no trouble fishing other types of waters for other species of fish.

Let us take a trip to a small stream that we know holds trout and learn how to fish it. Conditions will vary from stream to stream, so we will look at a couple of common scenarios.

## The Meadow Stream

In such a stream, you can make unobstructed backcasts across the stream; no trees or bushes crowd the banks. You can fish without standing in the water as long as you can reach the fish with your fly. The water in this section has a flat and even flow from left to right with a depth of a few feet. If you were to stand in the water here, it might be over your head.

As you stand quietly on the bank, watching the stream, you notice that there is an occasional small plip, and a ring of disturbance forms on the surface just about 25 feet upstream to your left. The next rise is in about the same spot, just this side of midstream, about 6 feet out from the bank on which you are standing.

There is no obvious insect activity upon the water, no clearly visible armada of mayflies floating past you, no fluttering caddisflies skimming the surface. The trout seem to be opportunistically feeding on whatever drifts by. This is the perfect time to use your size 14 Adams. (If there *were* an apparent hatch in progress, your strategy would be to attempt to match whatever was hatching as closely as possible. When your arsenal of trout flies becomes a bit more sophisticated, that will be easier. Now, though, the Adams might still be the closest match for mayflies, while the Elk Wing Caddis would have to serve for a caddisfly hatch.)

Tie the Adams to your tippet and treat it with fly floatant (see chapter 10). Now, watch the spot where the trout has been rising, and note its location carefully. Because the bank is clear and the stream is unobstructed by boulders and snags, you should be able to stand right where you are and cast to the trout. You do not want to move any closer, because you may spook the fish. At least you know, by its regular feeding, that your presence at your present position is not alarming it.

Typically, the trout will not actually be where you see the rise. It is about 3 feet farther upstream, near the bottom, where the current is weaker, and it is watching the surface above and slightly farther upstream for food. When a potential tidbit comes into view, the trout slowly rises towards it, drifting downstream with it while it gives it a good inspection. The relatively relaxed pace of the flow in this stream affords it that luxury. If the stream were very fast, the trout would have to decide in a split second. In this stream, though, the trout will stay with the morsel for about 2 more feet. If it accepts it as food, it will sip it in at about the spot at which you have been seeing the rises. If not, it will let it drift by.

Observe, too, whether the rises vary much in their distance from the bank. In streams with a great abundance of food and a dense population of trout, individual trout will stake out a position near the bottom and feed only on insects that drift over that spot. These are called *feeding lanes*, and although this seems like a terribly limited method of acquiring food, a trout's efficiency is improved by sticking to a single feeding lane in times of plenty, rather than racing all over the stream chasing down morsels in competition with its neighbors. In streams with few trout and low competition, however, trout may forgo strict adherence to a single feeding lane and cover more ground.

You have noticed that the location of the rises is pretty uniform in this case. Your object, now, is to cast your Adams so that it lands on the water about 3 feet upstream of the spot where the rises occur and will drift naturally down directly over it. Because you are positioned on the bank so that your cast will be almost straight upstream, and because there are no complex currents in this part of the stream, you should have no problem achieving a drag-free float. That means the fly will drift naturally from where it lands on the water to at least the point where the trout should strike it. It will float along, without any sign of drag, at the exact speed of the water on which it rides.

Drag is caused by the fact that the whole stream of water, from bank to bank, is not flowing uniformly. A stream is made of many seams of currents running side by side at different speeds. These different seams are caused by differences in the bottom features of the stream, by objects hanging in the water, and by changes in the contours of the banks. Where the water flows over a submerged boulder, for example, a seam of slightly slower water develops because of the obstruction. The width of seams may vary from inches to feet. Often these individual seams are apparent to the observer. In the type of slow, deep stream you are fishing here, though, they are harder to see.

Drag on the fly, then, occurs when some part of your line or leader is being pulled at a different speed from your fly by another seam of current. If your line or leader lies upon a seam running slower than the seam upon which the fly sits, an S curve will form in the line. As the faster seam overtakes the slower one, the slower part will ultimately inhibit the progress of the faster part, and the fly will be dragged unnaturally. Conversely, if some part of the line is being pulled faster than the fly, the line and leader will straighten out, and the fly will be pulled faster than the seam on which it rides. In both cases, a tiny wake will appear behind the fly, and the trout will immediately know that there is something alarming about this situation. Not only will the trout refuse to eat the fly, but it may quit rising altogether, completely eliminating your chances of catching it for perhaps hours. This is called having ***put down*** the fish.

To overcome drag, the line must be manipulated either during or after the cast. A cast that lands with numerous, slack S curves intentionally put into it will allow the fly to travel farther without drag, as the curves act as absorbers of the different tensions on the line. Mending the line after the cast, as discussed in chapter 2 under rod length and chapter 4 under floating lines, also eliminates drag by correcting drag-causing bellies in the line as they develop.

Here, though, you have no drag problems. You cast your fly perfectly to the spot indicated and let it drift on the current back towards you. You must not, however, let much slack develop in your line, for if the trout strikes while you have a big belly in the line, you will not be able to set

S *curves in the line and leader allow a fly to drift farther before dragging.*

the hook; you will lift the rod and the fly will not be affected at all. Therefore, as the fly drifts towards you, strip in line with the hand not holding the rod. But strip no faster than the fly is drifting, or you will create your own drag. By allowing the line to pass between the rod grip and the hand holding it, you can strip in line with your free hand, drop the stripped line to the ground as you snub it against the grip with your rod hand, and reach once more for more line with your free hand. Thus, you keep up with the drift of the fly.

The fly drifts over the spot where the trout has been rising. Nothing happens. Let it drift another couple of feet. Because you have been taking up slack line, you can now simply lift the fly off the water, directly into a smooth backcast, make a couple of false casts to work the loops from the ground out through the guides, and lay down your forward cast exactly where you cast before. You do not want to lift the fly from the water too near the fish, for sometimes the lift is not perfectly smooth, and the resulting disturbance can spook the trout.

Now you let the fly make its drag-free drift once more, taking up the slack, and anticipating the strike. And there it is! The trout has sipped in the fly exactly where it has been rising. You lift your rod, holding the line tight against the grip so it does not slip and diminish the setting of the hook. And now the trout is on. You can feel its fight. But it is not large. You do not need to let line slip out to avoid breaking the tippet, and you will not need to play this one off the reel. Just continue to strip in line with your free hand, and bring the trout to the bank.

Well done! You have landed your first trout on a fly, the first of many, I hope. Take a moment to savor the experience; there will never be another first trout. Yet, for me, after having caught hundreds of fish on flies, the amazement of the strike has never lessened. That I can get a fish to come up to the surface and accept my counterfeit as authentic—I am still as astonished today as I was when I caught my first trout. Whenever it happens, no matter how confident I am about the outcome, it still seems like a miracle. I hope you will retain that sense of wonder as well.

But for now, back to the stream. What if you had gotten to the stream and there were no trout rising at all? You could still use a dry fly like the

Adams, casting it upstream and letting it drift back down, hoping to tempt some hungry fish into striking it. But you would have to be willing to make an awful lot of casts, hitting every potential feeding lane and waiting for the fly to drift back each time.

A better way is to explore with an underwater fly. Your Bead Head Woolly Bugger and Hornberg are ideal. In this stream, with the water moving slowly, the Hornberg is probably the best choice. If the water were faster, you would need the weighted fly in order to get deep enough. Still, if the Hornberg produces nothing after a few casts, switch to the Woolly Bugger and try again.

The procedure is a simple one. Cast the fly about 45 degrees across and downstream from where you are standing. Try to place the fly at about midstream. The current will sweep the fly, leader, and line downstream as the fly sinks below the surface. Begin stripping in line when the fly is straight downstream below you. If you feel nothing hit the fly, cast out a couple of feet farther into the stream and repeat the process, continuing until you have cast either to the opposite bank or as far as you are able. Next, move a few yards downstream and begin all over again, fishing in close at first, and then expanding your swing until you have covered the area to the extent of your reach.

You can also fish nymphs this way, as well as traditional wet flies and all types of streamers. Most often, the fish will hit just at the end of the swing, as you start stripping. Because you do not have to make sure the fly does not create drag on the surface, as when fishing a dry fly, you can cover a lot more ground fishing downstream with subsurface flies.

**The Woodland Stream**
The main difference between woodland streams and open-meadow streams is that the trees and bushes that always crowd the banks of woodland streams force you into the water. There is no other way to find room for a backcast except to stand in the stream away from the foliage. Often, too, woodland streams are boulder-strewn, presenting a more complex and challenging scenario than streams that meander through meadows.

Because you must get off the bank and into the water, it is especially important that you first take some time to watch the stream. You do not want to be sloshing right out into what may prove to have been the spot where all the fish were holding. Whether or not fish are rising, close observation will reveal the intricacies of this section of stream. The water is moving at a fairly good pace, this time from right to left, and its movement around and over the rocks creates a symphony of gurgles, hisses, tinkles, and roars that make it much more difficult to hear the small sounds of rising trout. You must, therefore, look carefully. Notice the way seams of current speed up as they squeeze between boulders and then stop and eddy behind them. See how smooth and clear the lip of water is just above the small rapids and how still it becomes just past the foamy commotion below. Observe how eddies form and curl along the banks. Note how difficult it would be to see a rise. Try to imagine what your fly, leader, and line will do on the water when you cast across some of those seams.

As far as you can determine, after several minutes of watching, there are no risers. There are, however, a number of small spots below boulders and riffles where you can see objects on the surface drift into a pocket, get trapped in an eddy momentarily, circle once or twice around the saucer-sized area, and get caught back in the current and swept downstream. Those are places of weaker current where trout can hold and give tidbits a more deliberate look. Those are the places you want to explore with a fly.

One way to do it is to fish downstream with your Bead Head Woolly Bugger. Here, the current is fast enough to require your fly to have some weight. Because the water is only knee-deep in most places, you can position yourself pretty well wherever you want. You will cast downstream but not too much across, depending on how many boulders and other obstacles will cause your line to hang up as it swings across the stream. Usually, you will be able to fish mostly straight downstream, and you must move your whole self farther left or right to change the lanes you are fishing. Rather than lengthening your casts, you can also move downstream as you fish, covering yards, perhaps miles, of water without ever making a cast longer than 20 feet. Keep in mind that as you strip line and drop it on the water during your retrieve, it will be swept downstream in an increasingly elongating loop as the fly gets closer. So you want to keep your casts short and minimize the amount of line you are using.

Another way to approach this stream is with a dry fly upstream. The Royal Wulff is the perfect choice. Once treated with floatant, the Wulff will stay afloat in fast water, and its white wings will keep it visible. Again, you want to keep your casts short, perhaps only 10 feet at times, because you do not want a lot of line on the water in these complex currents. The idea, here, is to make a short cast to the slick water just inches above each eddy, or pocket. Usually that means that you want your fly to land alongside a boulder so that the seam will carry the fly right into the pocket below. In a stream like this, trout do not follow the fly for 2 or 3 feet as they do in slow water. They must snatch the fly off the surface almost the moment it appears, else it will be gone in moments. In the meantime, though, the fly has to act naturally; it must not appear to be dragged suddenly out of the pocket. The trout knows the difference between the fly's being swept out by the current and being yanked out by some unnatural force. That means you must be careful not to have excess line lying across seams that will pull on the line and cause the fly to drag. The less line, the easier it is to mend. For longer casts, as the fly drifts back downstream towards you, you will have to strip line quite fast to keep up with the fly and prevent too much slack from forming between you and the fly. On very short casts, simply raising the rod from horizontal to vertical will handle much of the slack.

In fast pocket water like this it is also sometimes best to fish a dry fly downstream. By casting a foot or so upstream of your target and keeping your rod high as the fly lands, you can then lower your rod and let the fly, leader, and line all drift downstream a couple of feet together without causing drag over the targeted pocket.

On small, rocky woodland streams, you learn the benefits of getting in the water and positioning yourself to your advantage, rather than making long, troublesome casts.

In any case, keep in mind that your survival does not depend on your outcome, nor does your worth as a human being. You are new to this activity, you are in a lovely place, and you are going to learn something if you stay receptive. The errors you make, the experiences you record, and the enjoyment you feel during these first several attempts are key to your success in the future. So do not allow frustration to ruin this experience.

## HERE'S WHY THIS CAN GET MORE COMPLICATED

I have described, above, two scenarios out of an infinite number that you may encounter on trout waters alone, not to mention the environs of numerous other species that can be pursued with a fly rod. Trout are sought in moving waters as small as tiny headwaters that can be straddled while being fished, and as large as rivers that pound across wildernesses and move house-sized boulders hundreds of yards. They are sought in the plunge pools of waterfalls; the tailwaters of hydroelectric dams; in rivers that must be floated with boats; in streams obstructed by fallen trees; in streams with solid, sandy bottoms; and in streams whose beds are bottomless, sucking muck. And there are streams whose bottoms are so strewn with slick, uneven stones that to escape without a sprained ankle or barked shin is nearly impossible. All of these places pose their singular challenges, providing opportunities for fly fishers to apply their experience, understanding of the sport, and educated guesses to solving the problems they present. Here are some of the others.

### Still Water

These are typically lakes and ponds—waters that do not have flowing currents caused by gravity. Such places are inhabited by an abundance of species commonly pursued with a fly rod. These include some of the same species of trout found in streams—brook, brown, rainbow, and cut-throat trout—as well as lake trout and other cold-water species such as landlocked salmon, grayling, and whitefish. Warm-water lakes are the home of such game fish as largemouth and smallmouth bass (smallies are also commonly found in cold-water lakes and rivers), pickerel, and pike, and of such panfish as sunfish and bluegills, crappies, yellow perch, bull-heads, and carp.

Still waters, like moving waters, can be fished from a boat, from shore, or by getting into the water and wading the shallows. Usually your reach, when wading in a lake or pond, is severely limited by the depth. But fishing the shorelines can be surprisingly productive in shallow weed beds.

The gear you use for trout in streams is often all you need for still water, especially for panfish and still-water trout. An 8-weight outfit for casting larger bass bugs is most often the choice for bass anglers. The main difference between fishing streams and still water is that still water does not provide movement to the fly. Wind might, but that is not what you are after. What you need to do in still water is convince the fish that your fly is an edible living creature, and that usually is indicated by the creature's own movement. (The exception is when still-water trout are feeding on a hatch of mayflies. Then you want to cast to the risers and let your fly sit as still as a real mayfly.) To surface flies, you must impart some action, usually erratic twitches and sudden, quick movements that imitate the struggles of an injured prey. Predators love the weak, injured, crippled, and otherwise helpless, for they require the least energy expenditure and, therefore, the greatest net nutritional return. In addition, still-water fishing necessitates your attracting the fish to your fly (there is no moving water to act as a delivery system), and so a certain amount of commotion is wanted as advertising. Surface flies that pop or glug as they are retrieved are a popular style of lure on warm-water lakes.

As in streams, floating lines are used for dry flies as well as sinking flies, but greater depth is achieved with sink-tip lines, full-sinking lines, and weighted flies. Flies are cast out, allowed to sink, and retrieved errat-ically by stripping line in alternating short tugs and pauses. The reel comes into play rarely, although at times, big bass and pike can make some strong runs that are best handled from the reel.

### Salt Water—Inshore
Fly fishing in salt water is a relatively recent development that has quickly become popular. Fly fishers pursue saltwater species, such as

striped bass, bluefish, and several small tuna species, while standing in the surf or from boats within sight of land; bonefish, tarpon, and permit while wading on shallow, saltwater flats or casting from flats skiffs; and marlin, swordfish, and sailfish well offshore from seaworthy boats. Sharks, wahoo, cobia, barracuda, sea trout, redfish, and even cod, haddock, halibut, and flounder have been taken on flies, to mention only a few.

Fishing in salt water presents a whole new set of concerns, including waves, surf, and tides. Inshore game fish are often most active during certain stages of the tide cycle. Wading saltwater anglers must be especially aware of the tides, as accessibility to good fishing areas may be limited to low tide.

Inshore fly fishing from a boat in salt water is not much different from fly fishing from a boat in fresh water. Most often, an outfit somewhat heavier than the 5-weight trout gear is used—a 9-weight is a good choice—and an intermediate line, rather than a floating line, will sink just a couple of inches beneath the surface and be less affected by wind and wave action. Perhaps the most common problem encountered when fly-fishing from a boat is keeping your line from catching on everything in sight and avoiding standing on it during a cast. As when fly-fishing anywhere, retrieval of the fly requires your stripping line and dropping the slack in loops at your feet. You will be amazed at how often you will shift your feet unconsciously and find that your next cast is violently abbreviated by the fact that you are now standing on the line and keeping it from shooting through your rod guides. If not that, you will be continually entertained by your line's ability to find protruding objects to loop itself around while you are trying to lay out a nice, long cast, and the result will, again, be a joltingly truncated affair. Nonetheless, fishing inshore waters from a boat will afford you the greatest mobility, as it allows you to quickly investigate areas of bird activity, which indicates baitfish concentrations, which in turn is usually the locale of feeding game fish.

Fly fishing from shore in salt water necessitates your getting into the water a little way. Because of wave action on the beach, whether at high tide or low, any attempt to stay dry will inevitably put you too far from productive water, no matter how well you can cast. You must wade out as far as you dare so that your casts will reach out as far as possible beyond where the sand is exposed by each receding wave. This means that you will be standing in a section of the surf where releasing your retrieved loops of stripped line will be like dropping them in a sand-filled blender set on puree. On your next cast, instead of shooting several yards of line through your rod guides, a large and tangled rat's nest will rise from the foam and be stopped by the very first guide.

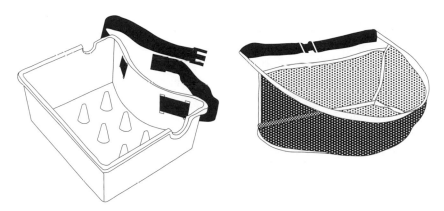

*Stripping baskets come in the form of plastic tubs (left) or mesh baskets. The cones molded into the bottom of the tub help keep loops of line from tangling.*

Most fly fishers who frequent the surf use a ***stripping basket*** to remedy that problem. Stripping baskets take many inventive forms but are all basically a small washtub held at the hip by waist and shoulder straps into which your stripped line can be dropped. On the next cast, the loops will flow from the basket unhindered and without tangles.

Fly fishing from the surf is a fine and popular way to pursue striped bass, bluefish, bonito, amberjack, mackerel, and a number of other inshore game fish. Here, again, a 9-weight outfit with intermediate line is preferred. Inshore fishing usually involves a lot of blind casting, but there are times when you will be casting to visible schools of fish.

### Salt Water—Flats

These are shallow, tidal areas in the tropics where bonefish, permit, and tarpon ghost through crystalline, sparkling waters in search of prey. Most common in the Bahamas, Florida Keys, Belize, and Venezuela, as well as Christmas Island in the Pacific Ocean, tropical flats are most commonly fished by wading or from a specially designed flats skiff that can maneuver in remarkably shallow water. The skiffs are equipped with a raised platform from which a guide poles the boat as close as possible to the quarry. The angler casts from the front deck, which is entirely free of anything that can catch the line during a cast. He can still stand on his line, however.

Flats fishing requires extreme stealth, for the water on tropical tidal flats is clear and shallow, and the fish are always cautious and wary. A bad cast can send an entire school of bonefish into a terrified and instant retreat. A hookup with a bonefish, permit, or tarpon, however, can turn your reel into a blur. All of these fish are fast, strong, and sustain remarkably long runs. Once hooked, they will take up all the slack line on the deck, set your reel spinning until all the fly line is gone, and run you well into the backing before slowing down. In addition to that demonstration of raw speed, common to all three species, tarpon will also jump, rocketing their entire length out of the water before crashing back and taking another blazing run. When a tarpon jumps, you must give it slack line so that it cannot throw the hook. This is called *bowing to the fish*.

There is no blind casting on the flats. Flats anglers stalk and cast to individual fish. Because the water on flats is not churning, wading fly fishers usually do not use stripping baskets.

### Salt Water—Offshore

This is deep-sea fishing. Anglers are most often well out of sight of land, sometimes on the Gulf Stream, in search of marlin, sailfish, and swordfish. This requires the heaviest fly-fishing gear and great endurance on the part of the angler. Hookless, feathered teasers are trolled behind the boat, over known feeding areas of these large predators. When a fish shows interest in the teaser, the lure is hauled in and the angler casts a large fly in its place. Once hooked, the fish will make long runs, spectacular bucking-bronco leaps, and deep dives. The fight can last hours. Offshore fly fishing has become enormously popular, with marlin weighing well over 200 pounds being landed on 20-pound tippets.

As you can see, there is no lack of fly-fishing opportunities, and I have only just skimmed the surface. The International Game Fish Association, which keeps the official tally of world record catches for all types of tackle, lists seventy-nine species of freshwater fish and ninety-three species of saltwater fish that have been caught on a fly.

# Chapter 9

# Waders

**FOR STARTERS**
**A bathing suit or shorts and a pair of sneakers**

Waders keep your clothes from getting wet while you stand in water. Sometimes, they keep you from developing hypothermia as well. If you are not standing in water while you fish—if you are fishing from a boat or from the bank—you do not need waders; you are not wading. If, however, you *are* wading, but the water is warm and you do not care if your clothes get wet, you do not need waders either. That is called *wet wading*, and some fly fishers prefer to wade wet, whenever possible.

I am, here, suggesting a compromise—a bathing suit or shorts and a pair of sneakers. If, however, you don't mind wading in a pair of jeans and hiking boots, go right ahead. The point is simply that I want you to start fly fishing with a minimum of paraphernalia and hassle. You definitely need a rod, reel, line, leader, and flies, which are already enough to deal with. If you can get away without having to acquire a pair of waders for now, my argument that fly fishing need not be a complicated, demanding pursuit will be all the more convincing. So do not worry about waders for now; just get into the water and fish. For safety, though, you may wish to glue felt soles, available at most fly-fishing specialty stores, to the bottom of your sneakers. They make walking on slippery stones much less hazardous.

## HERE'S WHY THIS CAN GET MORE COMPLICATED
Waders are handy because, with relatively little effort, you can slip them on over your clothes, wade in the water as long as you want, take them off when you are finished, and not have to hike back to your car and drive home in soaking wet pants. Some wader materials will also insulate your body against the devastating effects of standing in ice water for hours.

Although the advantages of using waders seem clear, even this piece of fly-fishing gear can overwhelm. First, there are two basic forms of waders—bootfoot and stockingfoot. Then there are at least three styles of each form—chest, waist-high, and hip waders. All of those are made in a variety of materials that vary in utility and price. And then there are the attendant gizmos and extras that help waders work better, most with variations of their own.

**Bootfoot Waders and Stockingfoot Waders**

Waders are basically a pair of waterproof pants. If you weld a rubber boot to the bottom of each leg, you can take off your shoes, slip your feet down through the legs and into the boots, hitch the waist above your belt and hold them up there with a pair of suspenders, and you have a watertight garment in which to walk in the water. Waders with boots attached to the bottoms of the legs are called *bootfoot waders*.

The advantages of bootfoot waders are that they are quick to get on and off and usually the less expensive option. Sometimes, those are the most important criteria. But bootfoot waders also have a few

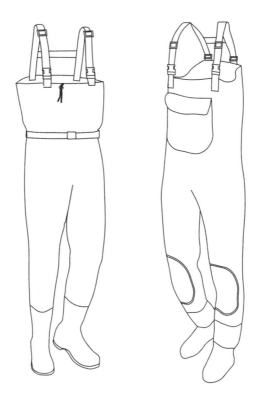

*These bootfoot waders* (left) *are made of a breathable material. The stockingfoot waders* (right) *are made of neoprene and require separate wading boots. Both pairs are chest waders.*

disadvantages. Even if they are the right size, rubber boots are unpleasant footwear in which to walk long distances. Bootfoot waders also offer little or no ankle support. When you are walking on a streambed strewn with irregularly shaped, slimy rocks of diverse sizes, bootfoot waders offer no protection from a twisted ankle. Muck bottoms, too, present a problem for bootfoot waders, for you are as likely to pull your foot out of the boot as pull your boot out of the muck.

Stockingfoot waders, on the other hand, are like the Doctor Denton–style pajamas that toddlers wear; the legs continue right down and form a closed foot. Although watertight, they cannot be worn without additional footwear because the bottoms of the feet are not meant to withstand that kind of wear. Wading boots, which look much like hiking boots, are worn over the feet of the waders.

The advantages of this arrangement exactly remedy the disadvantages of bootfoot waders: they are comfortable for walking, provide excellent ankle support, and are tightly secured to your feet. The disadvantages are that they take a while to get on and off and that you must buy boots as well as waders.

### Boot Soles

*A wading boot looks much like a hiking boot but usually has a felt-covered sole.*

This is a good time to mention that whether you use bootfoot waders or separate wading boots, there are a number of materials that may be applied to the soles to make them more effective on different bottoms. Felt is the most common sole, as it grips well on slick underwater surfaces. For extra traction on algae-covered stones, aluminum or carbide steel cleats may be added to the felt pads. The one disadvantage to felt is that it is somewhat absorbent, and unwanted microorganisms can be transferred among bodies of water. Felt soles are suspected of spreading the organism that causes the devastating whirling disease in trout. Some types of nonabsorbent rubber soles make excellent substitutes for felt and will accept cleats as well.

### Chest, Waist-High, and Hip Waders

Bootfoot waders and stockingfoot waders each come in three basic styles: chest, waist-high, and hip waders.

Chest waders come all the way up to your armpits. Suspenders are typically included, and there is often an inside pocket in the chest for a fly box and other items. Chest waders allow deep wading in surf, lakes, and rivers.

Waist-highs are waders that stop at the waist. They rarely have suspenders but are nearly always equipped with belt loops. Waist-highs are cooler than chest waders in hot weather.

Hip waders, also called hippers, are individual legs, unconnected to each other. On the outside top of each leg is a loop that attaches to your belt, keeping the hipper from falling down. For shallow streams, these are a convenient alternative to higher waders.

## Materials

A few years ago, before there were affordable microfibers, waders were made of either canvas or latex. They were heavy, hot, and awful. Upon removing them, you often found your clothing as wet from your own sweat as if you had not worn waders at all.

Today, there are a number of fibers that keep water from coming in while allowing perspiration to get out. These breathable fabrics are the

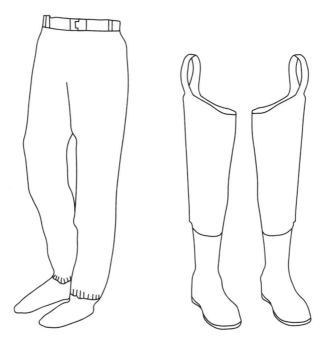

*These waist-high waders* (left) *are stockingfoot models, while the hip waders* (right) *are bootfoot models. The opposite arrangement is also available.*

predominant material of which waders are made. They are light, comfortable even in hot weather, durable, and can be used for bootfoot as well as stockingfoot models.

Neoprene, the stuff wetsuits are made of, is an excellent material for cold weather waders. Neoprene waders usually fit quite snugly, so they, unlike other waders, are normally worn over only long johns rather than street clothes.

It is still possible to find some ultra-lightweight nylon waders that are compact and inexpensive. They will usually last only about one season, though, because they are not durable. Although lightweight, they lack the breathability of waders made of the newer fibers and tend to allow sweat and condensation to soak your clothes.

### Fit

The only people who look good in waders are those who look good in absolutely anything. The other 99.9 percent of the population look silly when wearing waders, and there is nothing that can be done about it. Waders are not meant to make a fashion statement; they are meant to be practical. To that end, waders should fit you well enough so they are not overly baggy. You want to be somewhat hydrodynamic so that you do not present more surface area than necessary for moving water to press upon. On the other hand, you do not want your waders (except neoprene) so taut that you cannot bend your knees high enough to step over a log or, more importantly, climb out of the river.

No matter what your size and shape, you can find waders to fit you. There are waders designed especially for women, sizes for children, and even, somehow, waders with a built-in fly for convenience. Just be sure not to judge their utility by how you look in them.

### Extras

There are a few things that can help your waders last longer, improve your safety, and make you more comfortable. Safety first. When wearing chest waders, you will want to wear a belt around your waist on the outside of the waders. Some chest waders have belt loops, but most do not. Either way, cinch some kind of web belt around the waders to keep water from filling them up in case you take a spill. Flat nylon webbing, like the strips from which lawn chairs are made, fitted with a plastic buckle makes an excellent wading belt. Take this precaution seriously; falling down and having your waders fill with water can be fatal.

Some streams, because of their bottom topography more than the speed or depth of their water, can be treacherous to wade. A staff of some

*This wading staff is collapsible, its sections strung together by bungee cord.*

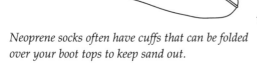

*Neoprene socks often have cuffs that can be folded over your boot tops to keep sand out.*

sort will afford you extra support and keep you from losing your balance and breaking your limbs or your rod. Wading staffs can be simply a stick that you pick up off the ground, or you can buy a staff that collapses down to a conveniently portable size and expands, when you need it, to 4 or 5 feet of sturdy aluminum tubing.

Comfort can be improved, whether you use bootfoot or stockingfoot waders, by slipping a pair of neoprene socks over your feet (over either your regular socks or bare feet) before putting your feet into your boots. If your stockingfoot waders already have neoprene feet, you won't need these. The neoprene socks, sometimes called booties, perform a number of functions. They cushion your feet, which can take a pretty tough beating on stony bottoms. They provide an extra layer of effective insulation against cold water. And they protect lightweight stockingfoot material from wearing out inside your boots.

When fishing in surf or streams with sandy bottoms, grit can easily get inside your wading boots and wear out the stockingfoot material, which will cause the waders to leak. To remedy that, some neoprene socks have a built-in cuff that folds over the top of the boot to seal out sand. Most modern stockingfoot waders have such cuffs built onto the legs at just the right height to fold down over your boot tops.

The extras above relate only to wading. Next we will look at some accessories that have more to do with actual fishing.

# Chapter 10

# Accessories

**FOR STARTERS**
**A small box for carrying your flies; some fly floatant;**
**and a pair of line clippers**

You now have a rod, a reel, line, a leader, ten flies, a stream in which to fish, and something to wear while wading. You are almost ready to try your luck. All you need now is some kind of *box* in which to carry your flies. It really does not matter much what kind of box it is for now, but at some point you will want to buy a box made for carrying flies. Such boxes have a few characteristics that make them better than the random pill bottle, matchbox, or candy tin. First, a good fly box stays securely closed, yet is easy to open. When you are standing out in the stream, holding your rod under your arm, you do not want a container that is difficult to open, especially if it opens with a jolt and pops your flies out into the river. You also do not want a container that will allow all your flies to blow away when you open it in the wind. Additionally, the container should give you easy access to individual flies; you do not want to have to dump all of them into your palm in order to select one, nor do you want a whole intertwined mass of flies to come out at once. And you want a box that will stay afloat if you drop it in the water, even if you have to chase it downstream for fifteen minutes. Fly boxes are designed with all that in mind. It is also a good idea to put your name and phone number or e-mail address on your fly box to increase the possibility of getting it back when you do lose it to the current or leave it on a rock, as most of us inevitably do.

*This clear plastic fly box has compartments for different types or sizes of flies.*

*Gel-type floatants come in small plastic squeeze bottles.*

The *fly floatant* will be necessary when you want to use your dry flies—the Royal Wulff, Adams, Elk Wing Caddis, Dave's Hopper, and Muddler—and keep them on the surface. Most dry flies that are tied well will float for a little while without being treated with floatant. After a while, though, they will begin to get waterlogged and lose their perky buoyancy. It is best, therefore, to treat them with floatant when you first tie them on. Then they will behave well for a long time. Floatant comes in a number of forms: powder, spray, gel, paste, solid, and liquid. For now, I recommend the gel. This comes in a half-ounce squeeze bottle and looks like petroleum jelly. After you tie your dry fly to your tippet, squeeze a small dollop, the size of a pea, onto your fingertip and squeeze it with your thumb. Your body heat will cause it to liquefy. When it becomes runny, rub it all over the fly, being careful not to hook yourself. Fluff the fly back into its original fuzziness, and you are ready to roll.

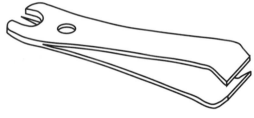

*Your clippers are the tool you will use the most. They usually come with a tiny point for clearing out the eyes of hooks and a hole so you can hang them on a zinger.*

The *line clippers* are for cutting your tippet when you want to change flies and for snipping off the tag ends of knots. Line clippers are similar in design to fingernail clippers, in that their two opposing cutting blades meet each other edge to edge, rather than slicing past each other like the blades of scissors. This allows them to cut even the thinnest tippet materials.

For now, that is all you need.

### HERE'S WHY THIS CAN GET MORE COMPLICATED

In almost no time at all, possibly even the next time you go fishing, you will add to that simple list of accessories. That is because many accessories are handy items that improve your fishing experience. Others serve only to load you down with things that looked good in the store, but have proved to be something you will use once in a lifetime, if that. Of the former, there are several useful things you will want to accumulate once you decide that you are going to stick with fly fishing.

**Fly Boxes**

One of the first things you will find as you continue to fly-fish is that you need more flies, not simply to replace the ones you left in trees or snapped off with a poorly timed cast, but more *kinds* of flies—more patterns, sizes, and colors. You will notice that the fish are eating something that your current stock of flies does not imitate. Or you will come upon an angler who is catching fish while you are not, and he or she may be kind enough to share the name of the successful fly, one you will want to acquire. Or you will read an article in which the author suggests some patterns that have worked well. Or you will be in a fly shop, mesmerized by the beauty and abundance of the hun-
dreds of flies you do not own, and you will vow to begin remedying your deficit on the spot. Or, eventually, all of the above. In any case, your lone fly box soon will be inadequate to hold all your flies.

*A fly box made of rippled foam. The ripples keep dry-fly hackles from being flattened when the box is closed.*

If you fish for different species, such as trout and bass, you will want separate boxes for your bass bugs and trout flies, at the very least. But even if you fish only for trout, sooner or later you will want to separate your dry flies from your wet flies. Then you may want separate boxes for mayflies and caddisflies, nymphs and streamers, bucktail streamers and feathered streamers. You can divide almost endlessly, depending on your penchant for organiza-
tion. Clearly, though, you will be accumulating fly boxes.

There are an awful lot of designs for fly boxes. Some are just boxes divided into compartments in which several different patterns, or several sizes of the same pattern, can be stored. Other types of boxes are lined with foam or cork into which you may poke the hook points. Thus, each fly sits individually wherever you pin it. Yet other boxes, made for nymphs and streamers, contain metal clips under which you slide the hook bend so that, again, each fly is held individually. There are boxes that combine these designs, opening like a book, with one side lined with foam or divided into little compartments for dry flies, and the other side having clips for nymphs and streamers. (You do not want to put dry flies

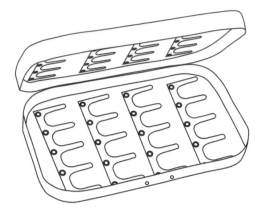

*Aluminum boxes with metal clips are designed to hold streamers, nymphs, and wet flies.*

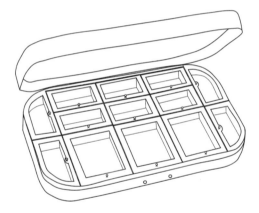

*This expensive aluminum box has compartments with individual see-through doors.*

under the clips, because the bristly hackle collars will flatten from being pressed against the box.) Some dry-fly boxes open like a book and contain individual compartments, each with its own spring-loaded door. When you open the box in the wind, you do not expose the entire contents to danger.

Some fly boxes are made of plastic, some of aluminum, and some of Styrofoam. Some are held closed by friction, some by springs, and some by magnets. Some are watertight and will float forever (a good thing), while at the same time not allowing your flies to dry (a bad thing). Boxes also come in many sizes. Some are large because they are designed to hold large flies, such as those for bass and saltwater species. Others are large because they are designed to hold a lot.

It is impossible for me to suggest the right types of boxes for you. I have tried nearly every kind and find most of them useful for something, if only for storing extra flies at home. Which types you prefer will depend upon your personality, the intended use, and any number of things. As with everything in fly fishing, once you come to understand the sport, the daunting plethora of choices will suddenly become a pleasant opportunity for you to find exactly what you want.

### Vests

Once you begin accumulating fly boxes, you will need more pockets in which to carry them. A fishing vest is just the thing, for it affords you a hands-free way to take all your paraphernalia out into the stream with you, is short enough to not get wet (usually), and can be organized in such a way that you will be able to find the right box when you need it.

Most good vests are made with several pockets of different sizes, especially for holding fly boxes. They also have pockets for carrying spools of tippet materials, extra leaders, sunglasses, raingear, extra spools for your reel, bug dope, lunch, and assorted other things that we will get to later. Most vests are also equipped with a couple of D-rings to which some of those assorted things may be attached. Many vests also come with a small fleece patch on which to hang your used flies to dry.

*A typical fly-fishing vest.*

Because of the amount of stuff that can be carried in a fly vest, weight can become a factor, and good vests are designed with features that reduce the effects of that weight on your enjoyment of being on the stream. Built-in yokes across the shoulders, as well as cushioned collars, greatly lessen the fatigue of wearing a loaded vest all day. Some vests, too, are made partly of a breathable mesh that makes them more comfortable to wear on hot summer days.

If you are fishing from a boat, you do not need a vest, necessarily, but you still need something that will keep all your gear together. There are a number of boat packs and chest packs made for the purpose, most of which are based very much on the idea of the vest. These packs, although not exactly garments, possess many pockets and compartments that perform precisely the same function as those in a fly vest. The chest pack is worn like a backwards backpack or fanny pack, and the boat pack is often designed to hang on a gunwale or a canoe strut so that it will stay accessible and dry.

One other alternative is the lanyard. This is for those who like to go as unencumbered as possible. It is basically a necklace made of a leather shoelace, or other type of cord, and strung with large beads as separators. After every few beads hangs a safety-pin-type fishing swivel to which you can fasten a clipper, a forceps, a holder for floatant, a couple of spools of tippet material, and even a little fly box.

## Nets

A net makes it easier to land some fish. I rarely use one. In fact, the only fish I can think of for which I regularly use a net is northern pike. These are big, crazy fish with big, sharp teeth, and the use of a net is more to

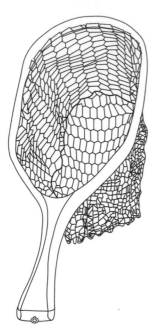

*A net for landing trout.*

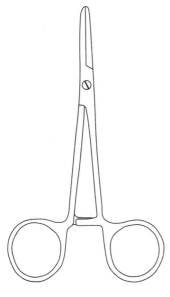

*Forceps are useful for removing hooks.*

keep the fish from harm than myself. Largemouth and smallmouth bass are easily landed by lifting them by the lower lip. Panfish can be held in the hand. Large saltwater fish are either gaffed if they are to be eaten, lifted by hand, or cut loose. Trout are the fish most often landed with a net, although there are two schools of thought on this.

Some anglers feel that when a trout is to be released, it has more likelihood of surviving its struggle if it is not handled at all. They feel that handling removes protective slime from parts of the trout's body and gives infections and fungi places of access. Others, however, feel that if a trout is handled carefully with wet hands, the slime is undisturbed, and less harm is done than is caused by contact with the frame and mesh of a net. More research needs to be done on the subject, but I tend to favor the simplicity of the hand-landing method and eliminate one other thing to carry.

There is, though, a decided appeal to some trout nets. If you are drawn to the beauty of such things as canoe paddles, wooden boats, snowshoes, and things crafted from hardwoods, trout nets are often right up there. Trout nets are typically attached by a retractable cord to a D-ring on the back of your vest's collar. When you need the net, you reach behind and pull the net around to the front. It remains tethered to the ring in case you drop it. When you let go, the retractor pulls the net around to its resting place at your back.

### Catch-and-Release Tools
Even if you are not planning to release your catch, you will still want to get your fly back. But when you wish to release a fish with as little stress on it as possible, these tools are especially useful. The most common device is the forceps or surgical hemostat, which acts as a tweezer clamp and can grasp and extract even the smallest hook without harming the fish. Other devices for

quick and harmless hook extraction are available as well.

## Fly-Drying Tools

Once you catch a fish with a dry fly, the fly becomes noticeably slimy and loses its ability to float high and dry. At that point, you cannot simply treat it again with floatant. First, you must restore it to its original condition. One way to do that is to bury it in a container of powdered silica crystals, which removes the slime, dries the fly, and restores flotation. Another way, which I prefer, is to squeeze the fly between two pieces of a substance called amadou. This is prepared from a type of fungus and has been used historically as tinder and as a surgical styptic. It is made available to fly fishers in the form of a pair of leather-backed pads, which absorb the moisture and slime from saturated flies and restore them to their original condition in seconds.

## Sinkers

Just as you will need floatant to make your dry flies float, you will sometimes need substances to make your wet flies sink. Whether

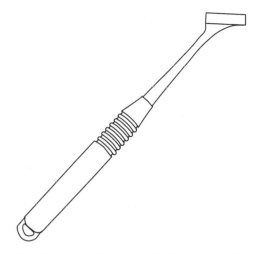

*The Ketchum Release is another hook-removal tool.*

*Amadou is a fly-drying medium that typically comes in a small leather book.*

because of swift current or deep holes, getting a fly down faster or deeper is often the key to catching fish. Various sizes of tiny split shot can be attached to your tippet or leader. Nowadays, these little weights are available in nontoxic materials instead of lead, which is a danger to wildlife and the environment.

Added weight also comes in the form of putty, which can be pinched out of a small container in the exact quantity you want. You then mold the putty around your leader. When you no longer need the weight on your

*Sink putty comes in a small plastic tub about the diameter of a half-dollar.*

line, you can peel it off and put it back in its container to be reused another time.

Another item in this category is called Mud. This is used to remove the shiny finish from leaders and make them sink. When you are fishing for extremely wary fish in clear, calm water, a leader that floats in the surface film may spook the fish not only with its flash, but also with the disproportionately large shadows it casts on the bottom. A little Mud rubbed on the leader takes care of the problem to a great extent.

**Strike Indicators**

When fishing nymphs along the bottom of a stream, it is often difficult to detect a strike. This is partly because the nymph, when fished most effectively, is drifting naturally with the current on a slack line, and partly because trout often take nymphs quite delicately. A trout can mouth your nymph and spit it out again without your ever realizing you had a strike. To remedy that, a highly visible indicator of some kind is attached high up on the leader, far enough from the nymph so that while the nymph is drifting down near the bottom, the indicator is still visible on the surface.

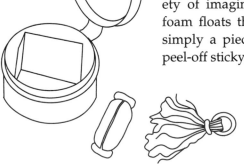

All the indicator does is make any change in the nymph's natural movement more obvious. If the indicator suddenly stops, slows, speeds up, or changes direction, set the hook.

Strike indicators are usually high-visibility, fluorescent pink or chartreuse and come in a variety of imaginative forms. Some are small, oval foam floats that twist onto the leader. Some are simply a piece of nonabsorbent yarn. There are peel-off sticky-tabs that fold around the leader, and there are floating putties that you mold onto the line. Nearly all make nymph fishing far more successful than no indicator at all.

*Strike indicators come in a variety of forms: putty* (left), *which comes as a cube in a small tub; twist-on foam pellets* (middle); *and tufts of yarn* (right).

**Zingers**

It should be apparent by now that you can end up carrying a fair number of tools and other gear with you when you go fly fishing. At one time or another, much of it actually proves useful, and the things that are most often used—clipper, forceps, floatant—need to be kept especially handy. Trying to dig them out of a pocket with one hand, while trying to control a thrashing fish with the other, is anything but relaxing. Zingers make those items as accessible as possible. A zinger is a button-sized housing containing a foot or two of spring-loaded cord. The housing attaches to the outside of your vest, and you can clip any tool to the snap swivel on the end of the cord. Normally, the tool dangles close under the housing within easy reach. When you need to use it, you just grab it; the cord extends and then yanks the tool safely back to its resting place when you let go. There are a few variations on zinger design, but all are intended to hold an item securely while keeping it handy.

*Zingers keep your most frequently used tools right where you need them.*

## Miscellany

The list above has by no means exhausted the items you will encounter that can become necessary to enhancing your fly-fishing pleasure. Depending on the degree to which you are absorbed in the sport, the paths you take in your progress, your age and physical condition, and which of the nearly endless aspects of fly fishing catches your fancy, you may find delight in using some of these miscellaneous items, or you may never have the slightest interest in any of them.

A *stream thermometer* may come in handy if you keep track of surface temperatures to determine breeding periods and other temperature-related phenomena.

A *hook sharpener* is always a handy item to have on the stream. This may be a simple, small sharpening stone, a diamond file, or a battery-operated grindstone.

A *penlight* is necessary if you are fishing at night. Changing flies in the dark is just about impossible. Several small lights are made especially for hands-free operation. Some clip to a pocket of your vest and have adjustable heads so that you can aim the beam where you want it and have your hands free to tie knots. Another type is held between the teeth, so that biting down turns the switch on and off.

*A stream thermometer.*

If you are of the age when your close-up vision is getting a bit soft, you may want to carry a *magnifier* also. There are magnifying glasses that

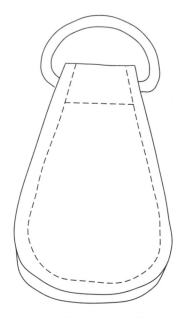

clip to the bill of your cap, as well as some combination magnifier-and-light gizmos.

A *leader straightener* can come in handy when your leader is badly coiled from being wound around your reel for a while. Pulled between two pads of rubber in a leather holder, the nylon leader heats up from friction and relaxes, straightening out to lie neatly on the water. The same can actually be accomplished by pulling the leader through your fist, but you can burn yourself from the heat produced.

Some people have a lot of trouble tying knots. There are *knot-tying tools* by the dozen to help you tie nail knots, blood knots, clinch knots, and surgeon's loops.

There are *stomach pumps* and *insect nets* to help you determine what the trout are eating. The stomach pump is similar to a small turkey baster and is used to extract the stomach contents of a trout in order to identify the hatch upon which it is feeding. The insect net is used to sweep the surface of the stream for the same purpose.

*A leader straightener is a small leather book containing two patches of rubber. When you draw your curled leader through the rubber, you generate enough heat to relax the curls.*

There are *micrometers* for measuring the diameter of your leader, *tweezers* for extracting tiny flies from your fly box, *threading devices* for guiding your tippet through tiny hook eyes, and probably many more things of which I will be reminded when I mine the pockets of my vest for long-forgotten gadgets.

# Conclusion

If you have read only the For Starters section of each chapter, you should by now appreciate that fly fishing is no more complicated than conventional fishing, golf, driving a car, or using a computer to write letters or pay your bills. All you need is the proper equipment and an understanding of what it is for.

If you have gone on to read the rest of each chapter, you now understand why fly fishing looked so unfathomable to you in the first place, and you have a sense of how wonderfully absorbed you can become in its vast richness if you so choose. Fly fishing, as you can see, may quite naturally lead to interests in physics, entomology, ecology, hydrodynamics, ichthyology, conservation, stream biology, botany, oceanography, marine biology, fly tying, and rod building. And those are only the obvious connections.

Another thing I hope you will realize, once you have read the entire book, is that the accoutrements of fly fishing can also be as simple and spare, or as complex and numerous, as you wish. Fly fishing helps you gain insight into your own personality. You may find that you are a minimalist, eschewing anything that is not truly essential. You acquire little gear, because you like to do as much as possible with as little as possible. You like to travel light. On the other hand, you may be someone who believes in being prepared for all eventualities. "Better safe than sorry" is your watchword. For you, a fishing vest with sufficient pockets has yet to be invented. You love gadgets and gizmos, and the inconvenience of having to carry everything around with you is nothing compared to the anguish of finding yourself in need of something you did not bring.

You may even find that you vary from one tendency to the other. Many fly fishers, myself among them, go through phases, like the natural ebb and flow of droughts and floods, dearth and plenty. I start out carrying everything I own and acquire, but soon realize that all that stuff is heavy and I rarely use most of it. That sets me off on a "lean and mean" campaign until I find myself wishing I had brought something I had eliminated from my kit, which starts a new accumulation phase, and so on.

Similar to that is the "general vs. detailed" struggle, or the "macro vs. micro" views. These manifest themselves in the levels of minutiae to which you will pursue particular aspects of fly fishing. Whereas one angler may have half a dozen fly boxes filled with imitations of each species of nymph in the Northeast, as well as each stage of those nymphs upon which trout feed, plus flies that imitate anomalous conditions of each of those nymphs, including cripples and emergers stuck in their nymphal shucks, another may feel sufficiently equipped when carrying only a nondescript, light-colored nymph and an equally universal dark one.

Likewise, some anglers are perfectly happy to use their equipment just as it comes from the manufacturer, while others cannot help but modify everything to their liking, from reshaping the cork on their rod grips, to rebuilding their leaders, to trimming the hairs on their flies.

There is no right or wrong way among those types. Fly-fishing enjoyment is not measured in the numbers or sizes of fish you catch. The true joy of fly fishing derives from the exceptional number of ways you can gain pleasure from it.

In order to continue deriving pleasure from fly fishing, however, all of us must strive to protect the waters we fish and their inhabitants from abuse and destruction. I am not one who frowns upon anglers' keeping their catch for food, but I am troubled when fish are killed for trophies and other forms of frivolous waste. As abundant as fish seem, there really are not enough to sustain wholesale killing by tens of millions of (licensed) anglers for long. As rich as fly fishing is in peripheral activities, when the fish are gone, the sport becomes meaningless.

One way to preserve the resource is to use barbless hooks on your flies. Barbless hooks do not preclude your landing fish and keeping them for food, but they do make it significantly easier to release the fish you do not wish to keep. Barbless hooks, as you would expect, often slip right out of a fish's lip when tension on the hook is relaxed. At worst, the fly may be grasped and pulled out without your ever having to handle the fish at all. This greatly increases the fish's chance of survival.

Flies tied on barbless hooks are available from fly dealers. You can also make regular hooks barbless by squashing down the barb with a pair of needle-nose pliers or, on small flies, with forceps. I urge you to do so.

Not only is it better for the fish, it makes it easier to set the hook. For the most part, you should lose no more fish than on barbed hooks.

By learning to fly-fish, you are joining a very large number of similarly smitten people. It is therefore important that you preserve the resource, protect the environment, be respectful of fellow anglers (one of them is me), and enjoy yourself for the rest of your life.

# Index

*Page numbers in italics indicate illustrations.*